CW00401413

THE UPGRADE KETO AIR FRYER

COOKBOOK

1000 Days of Healthy And Simple low
carb Recipes to Heal Your body & help
lose weight, Easy to make less than
30minutes

John k. Acosta

Table of contents

INTRODUCTION

In the dazzling pages of this Keto Air Fryer Cookbook, leave on a culinary excursion that melds the standards of the ketogenic way of life with the comfort and development of air broiling. As the enticing smell of healthy, low-carb fixings fills your kitchen, you'll find a mother lode of luscious recipes carefully created to line up with your well-being and health objectives.

This presentation makes way for a gastronomic experience, welcoming both beginner and prepared gourmet experts to investigate the harmonious connection between the ketogenic diet and the air fryer. From a perspective of innovativeness and dietary care, this cookbook tries to rethink your way of dealing with cooking, showing the way that tasty, fulfilling feasts can coincide flawlessly with a promise to low-carb living.

Inside these pages, expect a different cluster of recipes that rise above the limits of customary dietary limitations, embracing the idea that guilty pleasure need not undermine your well-being. From fresh and delicious air-broiled meats to lively, vegetable-forward manifestations, each dish is a demonstration of the amicable mix of taste and nourishment.

As you dig into the parts ahead, drench yourself in the viable tips, clever direction, and culinary insight that go with every recipe. This Keto Air Fryer Cookbook isn't simply an assortment of dishes; an aide enables you to make informed decisions about your dietary process. Whether you're looking for weight the executives, expanded energy, or essentially a tasty takeoff from the common, this cookbook entices you to embrace the extraordinary force of ketogenic cooking with the cutting-edge wonder that is the air fryer. Welcome to a domain where well-being cognizant cooking meets the craft of enjoying each significant piece.

In the pages that follow, you'll track down a variety of carefully organized recipes intended to take special care of different preferences and inclinations. From breakfast enchants that stir your faculties to exquisite lunch and supper choices that reclassify the limits of low-carb fulfillment, this cookbook offers a thorough cluster of dishes reasonable for any event.

Past the culinary domain, this book fills in as a confided-in buddy on your keto venture, giving an abundance of data on fixing choices, healthful bits of knowledge, and cooking procedures well-defined for the air fryer. Whether you're a culinary fan anxious to explore or a bustling individual looking for speedy, well-being-cognizant dinners, these recipes find some kind of harmony among effortlessness and connoisseur pizazz.

As you navigate through these culinary scenes, be propelled by the flavors as well as by the extraordinary capability of the ketogenic way of life. The presentation establishes the vibe for an all-encompassing way to deal with prosperity, underscoring that a pledge to well-being needs not penance but the delight of guilty pleasure.

In the core of this cookbook, find a culinary safe house where the standards of keto residing and the flexibility of air searing unite. Every recipe is a demonstration of the conviction that feeding your body can be a pleasant, tasty experience. Thus, fix your cover strings and set out on a culinary journey that rises above dietary limitations, celebrates imagination, and lifts how you might interpret what it means to enjoy each chomp genuinely. Your experience in the universe of keto-accommodating air searing is standing by.

Chapter 1: Getting Started with Keto

Beginning with the Keto diet includes understanding its standards, which principally center around devouring low-sugar, high-fat food varieties to prompt a condition of ketosis in the body. Start by finding out more about allowed and limited food sources — pick meat, fish, eggs, dairy, solid fats, and non-dull vegetables while staying away from grains, sugars, and high-carb things.

Compute your macronutrient proportions to guarantee you're fulfilling the guideline Keto rules, normally around 70-75% fats, 20-25% protein, and 5-10% carbs. Monitor your day-to-day consumption utilizing applications or food journals to keep up with the ideal equilibrium.

Consider bit by bit diminishing carb admission to limit the likely secondary effects, known as the "Keto influenza." Remaining hydrated and expanding electrolyte admission can lighten these side effects. Coordinate moderate activity, as it supplements the eating regimen's advantages.

Dinner arranging is vital — get ready Keto-accommodating recipes ahead of time to abstain from surrendering to high-carb enticements. Explore different avenues regarding assorted food choices to keep the eating routine supportable and agreeable.

Consistently screen your advancement by following weight, energy levels, and in general prosperity. Talking with a medical care proficient before beginning the Keto diet is fitting, particularly for people with existing ailments.

Generally, effective inception into the Keto way of life includes instruction, careful preparation, and a pledge to keep up with the endorsed macronutrient balance.

Figuring out Ketogenic Standards

Understanding ketogenic standards includes embracing the central ideas of a low-sugar, high-fat eating routine intended to prompt ketosis in the body. Ketosis happens when the body shifts from depending on glucose as its essential fuel source to consuming ketones, which are delivered from fats. Key standards incorporate confining carb admission to prompt this metabolic state, underlining utilization of sound fats, and directing protein consumption. Advantages might incorporate weight reduction, working on mental clearness, and improved energy levels. Be that as it may, it's significant to screen supplement consumption, remain hydrated, and talk with medical services before taking on a ketogenic way of life, as individual reactions can differ. Moreover, perceiving that the ketogenic diet may not be reasonable for everybody is fundamental to a nuanced comprehension of its standards.

Further investigation of ketogenic standards includes recognizing the science behind ketosis.

The body enters this state when glycogen stores are drained, prompting the expanded creation of ketones by the liver. Understanding macronutrient proportions is vital, regularly with an emphasis on a high level of fats (70-75%), a moderate measure of protein (20-25%), and negligible starches (5-10%).

Furthermore, perceiving the expected physiological variations and advantages is essential. Ketogenic counts of calories have been related to further developed insulin responsiveness, decreased aggravation, and upgraded fat digestion. Be that as it may, potential secondary effects like the "keto influenza" during introductory transformation, electrolyte lopsided characteristics, and lipid profile changes ought to be thought of.

A nuanced understanding includes recognizing wholesome ketosis for medical advantages and helpful ketosis, frequently utilized for ailments like epilepsy or neurodegenerative problems. Normal checking, customized changes, and a decent way to deal with micronutrient consumption add to a more complete comprehension of ketogenic standards.

Fundamental Fixings and Kitchen Apparatuses

Fundamental Fixings:

Flour: A flexible staple for baking and cooking.

Sugar: Adds pleasantness to sweets and balances flavors.

Salt: Upgrades taste and is an essential flavoring specialist.

Oils (Olive, Vegetable): Utilized in cooking and dressing.

Spices and Flavors: Raise dishes with profundity and fragrance.

Eggs: Tie fixings and add structure in baking.

Dairy (Milk, Spread, Cheddar): Key for lavishness and flavor.

Proteins (Meat, Fish, Tofu): Fundamental for a decent eating regimen.

Vegetables: Give supplements, varieties, and surfaces.

Kitchen Apparatuses:

Culinary expert's Blade: Adaptable for hacking and cutting.

Cutting Board: Safeguards surfaces and helps in food prep.

Blending Bowls: Fundamental for mixing and marinating.

Estimating Cups and Spoons: Exact fixing sums.

Pots and Skillet: Essential cookware for different dishes.

Spatula and Utensils: Help with flipping and taking care of food.

Whisk Integrates air into combinations for cushiness.

Baking Sheets and Dish: Vital for baking undertakings.

Grater: Shreds cheddar, vegetables, or zing.

Peeler: Eliminates skins from products of the soil.

Guarantee your kitchen is furnished with these fundamentals for a balanced culinary encounter. Try different things with flavors and procedures to find your exceptional cooking style.

Air Fryer Rudiments

Air fryers are flexible kitchen machines that utilize hot air dissemination to prepare food, giving a better option in contrast to customary broiling techniques. Here are a few critical parts of air fryer fundamentals:

1. How Air Fryers Work:

Air fryers use convection to circle hot air around the food, making a firm layer through the Maillard response.

The machine commonly has a warming component and a fan, guaranteeing even conveyance of intensity for predictable cooking.

2. Medical advantages:

Air fryers require insignificant or no oil, diminishing the general fat substance of the food contrasted with profound searing.

They offer a better choice for people who need the taste and surface of seared food with fewer calories and less oil retention.

3. Cooking Limit:

Air fryers come in different sizes, obliging various amounts of food. Consider the limit in light of your cooking needs and accessible counter space.

4. Adaptability:

Other than searing, air fryers can heat, meals, barbecue, and even warm extras, making them flexible for a scope of recipes.

A few models might have explicit presets for famous dishes, working on the cooking system.

5. Temperature and Time Control:

Air fryers permit exact temperature and time control, guaranteeing that different food varieties are cooked flawlessly.

Exploring different avenues regarding various settings can assist with accomplishing the ideal surface and flavor for explicit dishes.

6. Upkeep and Cleaning:

Most air fryers have removable, dishwasher-safe parts, making cleaning generally simple.

Ordinary upkeep, like cleaning the bin and checking for any oil buildup, keeps up with ideal execution.

7. Cooking Tips:

Preheating the air fryer can improve cooking results by guaranteeing even intensity dispersion.

Shaking or flipping food during the cooking system advances uniform firmness.

8. Normal Errors:

Overburdening the crate can prompt lopsided cooking, as the need might arise to course openly around the food.

Utilizing an excess of oil nullifies the point of air searing and may bring about a greasier surface.

9. Well known Recipes:

Air fryers succeed at cooking various food sources, including chicken wings, fries, vegetables, and even sweets like doughnuts or glazed donuts.

10. Contemplations while Purchasing:

Search for highlights, for example, flexible temperature settings, numerous cooking presets, and simple to-utilize controls.

Think about the apparatus' size, taking into account your kitchen space and cooking needs.

In outline, air fryers offer a helpful and better cooking technique, permitting people to partake in the freshness of seared food with diminished oil utilization. Figuring out their activity, trying different things with settings, and investigating assorted recipes can assist with amplifying the advantages of this advanced kitchen machine.

Ways to utilize an Air Fryer

Utilizing an air fryer can be a distinct advantage in the kitchen, giving a better option in contrast to customary broiling while at the same time keeping a heavenly taste and freshness. Here are a few hints to upgrade your involvement in an air fryer:

Preheat the Air Fryer:

Very much like a broiler, preheating your air fryer guarantees in any event, cooking and improved results. This step is especially significant for accomplishing a firm surface.

Utilize the Perfect Proportion of Oil:

While air fryers require less oil than customary searing strategies, utilizing a limited quantity of oil on your fixings can upgrade the firmness and flavor. Consider utilizing a cooking splash for an even coat.

Try not to Pack the Container:

To permit hot air to flow appropriately, try not to stuff the air fryer bushel. This guarantees that each piece of food gets equitably cooked and fresh.

Shake or Flip Part of the way Through:

For cooking, shake the crate or flip the food part of the way through the cooking time. This accomplishes a steady and brilliant earthy-colored surface.

Change Temperature and Time:

Recipes might change, so be adaptable to temperature and cooking times. Analysis to find the ideal settings for your #1 dishes, remembering that air fryers cook quicker than conventional strategies.

Use Material Paper or Container Liners:

To forestall staying and make cleaning more straightforward, consider utilizing material paper or bin liners. Guarantee they are ok for air searing and don't cover the whole crate to permit appropriate airflow.

Spritz with Water for Dampness:

To hold dampness in your food, gently spritz it with water previously or during the cooking system. This is especially valuable for things that might dry out without any problem.

Season Before Cooking:

Season your fixings before setting them in the air fryer to improve flavor. Marinades, rubs, and flavors can stick better to the food, making a more delectable outcome.

Explore different avenues regarding Various Food varieties:

Air fryers are flexible and can cook different food sources, from vegetables and proteins to sweets.

Try different things with various recipes to find the maximum capacity of your air fryer.

Clean Consistently:

Appropriate upkeep is fundamental. Clean the bushel, plate, and different extras after each utilization to forestall buildup development. Allude to the producer's directions for explicit cleaning rules.

Forestall Smoke:

A few food varieties might deliver more oil or fat, prompting smoke. To stay away from this, add a little water to the cabinet or utilize a trickle plate to get an overabundance of oil.

Proper Maintenance and Cleaning

Proper maintenance and cleaning are essential practices for the longevity and optimal functioning of various items, be it household appliances, vehicles, or personal belongings. Regular maintenance not only extends the lifespan of these items but also ensures their efficiency and safety.

In the realm of household appliances, routine cleaning prevents the buildup of dirt, dust, and grime, which can compromise performance and lead to malfunctions. For example, regular vacuum cleaner filter cleaning enhances suction power, while descaling a coffee maker maintains its brewing efficiency.

Vehicles require meticulous maintenance to operate smoothly and safely. Regular oil changes, tire rotations, and brake inspections contribute to overall vehicle health, reducing the risk of breakdowns and accidents. Additionally, keeping the interior and exterior clean not only preserves the vehicle's aesthetics but also protects it from corrosion and wear.

Personal items, such as electronic devices and tools, benefit from proper care. Cleaning screens and keyboards on devices prevents damage and ensures a clear display. Lubricating moving parts on tools maintains their functionality and prevents rust, contributing to their longevity.

In the context of homes, routine cleaning not only maintains a pleasant living environment but also safeguards against health hazards. Dusting, vacuuming, and disinfecting surfaces help eliminate allergens and harmful microorganisms. Proper maintenance of plumbing and electrical systems prevents leaks and potential hazards.

Beyond tangible items, personal hygiene and cleanliness play a crucial role in overall health. Regular bathing, dental care, and handwashing are fundamental practices that prevent illness and promote well-being.

In conclusion, proper maintenance and cleaning are integral to the functionality, safety, and aesthetics of various items in our lives. By incorporating these practices into our routines, we not only extend the life of our possessions but also contribute to a healthier and more efficient living environment.

Chapter 2: Keto Appetizers

Fixings:

1 pound of new Brussels sprouts

1/4 cup olive oil

1 teaspoon garlic powder

1 teaspoon onion powder

Salt and pepper to taste

1/2 cup ground Parmesan cheddar

Nourishment Data (per serving):

Calories: 150

Fat: 11g

Carbs: 7g

Fiber: 3g

Protein: 6g

Planning Time:

15 minutes

Cooking Time:

25 minutes

Servings:

4

Bearings:

Preheat the Stove:

Preheat your stove to 400°F (200°C).

Get ready Brussels Fledglings:

Trim the finishes of the Brussels fledglings and cut them down the middle.

Season with Goodness:

In an enormous blending bowl, throw the divided Brussels sprouts with olive oil, garlic powder, onion powder, salt, and pepper. Guarantee the fledglings are uniformly covered.

Spread on Baking Sheet:

Spread the carefully prepared Brussels sprouts on a baking sheet fixed with material paper, organizing them in a solitary layer.

Prepare Flawlessly:

Broil in the preheated stove for roughly 25 minutes or until the fledglings are brilliant brown and fresh on the edges.

Add Cheddar Sorcery:

Around 5 minutes before the Brussels sprouts are finished, sprinkle the ground Parmesan cheddar over them. Allow it to liquefy and shape a delectable outside layer.

Serve and Appreciate:

When the Brussels sprouts are cooked flawlessly, eliminate them from the broiler. Move to a serving platter and partake in this wonderful Keto starter.

Firm Zucchini Fries

Cooking Time: 20 minutes

Servings: 4

Fixings:

4 medium-sized zucchini

1 cup breadcrumbs

1/2 cup ground Parmesan cheddar

1 teaspoon garlic powder

1 teaspoon dried oregano

1/2 teaspoon salt

1/4 teaspoon dark pepper

2 enormous eggs

Headings:

Preheat the Broiler: Preheat your stove to 425°F (220°C). Line a baking sheet with material paper to forestall staying.

Plan Zucchini: Wash and trim the finishes of the zucchini. Cut them into meager strips looking like the state of conventional fries.

Make Breading Combination: In a shallow bowl, blend breadcrumbs, ground Parmesan cheddar, garlic powder, dried oregano, salt, and dark pepper. This will be the delightful covering for your zucchini fries.

Whisk Eggs: In another bowl, whisk the eggs until very much beaten. This will act as the limiting specialist for the breading.

Coat Zucchini Strips: Plunge every zucchini strip into the beaten eggs, guaranteeing an in any event, covering. Then, cover the strips with the breadcrumb blend, compressing the combination onto the zucchini to stick well.

Orchestrate on Baking Sheet: Put the covered zucchini strips on the pre-arranged baking sheet, leaving space between each piece for crisping.

Heat Flawlessly: Prepare in the preheated broiler for around 20 minutes or until the zucchini fries are brilliant brown and firm. Flip the French fries partially through to guarantee the two sides are cooked equally.

Serve Hot: Once finished, eliminate them from the stove and let them cool briefly. Serve the fresh zucchini fries hot with your most loved plunging sauce.

Nourishment Data (per serving):

Calories: 180

Complete Fat: 7g

Soaked Fat: 3g

Cholesterol: 90mg

Sodium: 480mg

Absolute Starches: 20g

Dietary Fiber: 3g

Sugars: 4g

Protein: 10g

Parmesan Garlic Wings

Planning Time: 15 minutes

Cooking Time: 45 minutes

Servings: 4

Fixings:

2 lbs chicken wings

1 cup ground Parmesan cheddar

4 cloves garlic, minced

1/2 cup unsalted spread, liquefied

1 teaspoon dried oregano

1 teaspoon dried basil

1/2 teaspoon salt

1/4 teaspoon dark pepper

1/4 teaspoon red pepper pieces (discretionary)

New parsley, cleaved (for embellish)

Bearings:

Preheat the Stove:

Preheat your stove to 400°F (200°C) and line a baking sheet with material paper.

Set up the Wings:

Perfect and wipe off the chicken wings with paper towels. Put them on the pre-arranged baking sheet.

Season the Wings:

In a bowl, blend ground Parmesan cheddar, minced garlic, dried oregano, dried basil, salt, dark pepper, and red pepper pieces if you lean toward some intensity.

Cover Wings with Combination:

Sprinkle liquefied margarine over the wings, it are equally covered to guarantee they. Then, at that point, sprinkle the Parmesan blend liberally over the wings, making a point to cover each piece.

Prepare Flawlessly:

Prepare the wings in the preheated stove for around 40-45 minutes or until they become brilliant brown and firm. Guarantee to flip the wings partially through for an even cook.

Trimming and Serve:

When the wings are cooked flawlessly, eliminate them from the stove. Sprinkle newly hacked parsley over the wings for an explosion of newness.

Appreciate!

Serve these tasty Parmesan Garlic Wings hot and partake in the crunchy, delightful goodness.

Nourishment Data (Per Serving):

Calories: 480

Protein: 28g

Fat: 38g

Carbs: 4g

Fiber: 0g

Sugars: 0g

Sodium: 620mg

Avocado Bacon Chomps

Planning Time: 15 minutes

Cooking Time: 15 minutes

Servings: 4

Fixings:

2 ready avocados, stripped and diced

1 cup regular flour

1 teaspoon baking powder

1/2 teaspoon garlic powder

1/2 teaspoon onion powder

1/2 teaspoon paprika

1/4 teaspoon cayenne pepper (change by taste)

Salt and pepper to taste

2/3 cup milk

1 huge egg

1 cup breadcrumbs

Oil for broiling

Bearings:

In a bowl, consolidate flour, baking powder, garlic powder, onion powder, paprika, cayenne pepper, salt, and pepper.

In a different bowl, whisk together milk and egg until very much consolidated.

Progressively add the wet fixings to the dry fixings, blending until you have a smooth player.

Tenderly overlap in the diced avocados, guaranteeing they are uniformly covered with the hitter.

In a shallow dish, spread out the breadcrumbs.

Heat oil in a griddle over medium intensity.

Utilizing a spoon, scoop bits of the avocado hitter and coat them in breadcrumbs, framing wastes.

Cautiously place the wastes into the hot oil, broiling until brilliant brown on the two sides.

Once fresh and brilliant, eliminate the squanders and put them on a paper towel-lined plate to ingest an overabundance of oil.

Serve the avocado wastes warm with your most loved plunging sauce.

Sustenance Data (per serving):

Note: Sustenance values are surmised and may change given explicit fixings utilized.

Calories: 250

Protein: 6g

Fat: 14g

Carbs: 28g

Fiber: 4g

Sugar: 2g

Cheddar and pepperoni cut

Fixings:

Pizza batter (locally acquired or natively constructed)

Pureed tomatoes

Mozzarella cheddar, destroyed

Pepperoni cuts

Olive oil

Italian flavoring (discretionary)

Planning Time:

15 minutes

Cooking Time:

12-15 minutes

Servings:

4 cuts

Nourishment Data (per cut):

Calories: 250

Protein: 12g

Fat: 10g

Carbs: 28g

Fiber: 2g

Bearings:

Preheat the Stove:

Preheat your stove to 475°F (245°C). If you have a pizza stone, place it in the broiler while it warms.

Carry Out the Mixture:

Carry out the pizza mixture on a floured surface to your ideal thickness. If you favor a slight hull, carry it out more; for a thicker covering, leave it a piece chunkier.

Set up the Pizza Base:

Move the carried-out batter to a pizza strip or a rearranged baking sheet fixed with material paper.

This will make it more straightforward to move the pizza into the stove.

Add Sauce and Cheddar:

Spread a fair layer of pureed tomatoes over the pizza batter, leaving a little line around the edges. Sprinkle a liberal measure of destroyed mozzarella cheddar equitably over the sauce.

Top with Pepperoni:

Put pepperoni cuts on top of the cheddar, dispersing them uniformly across the pizza.

Heat in the Broiler:

If utilizing a pizza stone, cautiously move the pizza to the preheated stone in the broiler. In any case, place the baking sheet straightforwardly on the stove. Heat for 12-15 minutes or until the hull is brilliant and the cheddar is effervescent and somewhat caramelized.

Wrap up with Olive Oil and Prepare:

When out of the broiler, shower the pizza with olive oil and sprinkle with Italian flavoring for an additional eruption of flavor.

Cut and Serve:

Permit the pizza to cool for a couple of moments, then, at that point, cut and serve. Partake in your natively constructed Cheddar and Pepperoni Cut!!

Avocado Fritters

On the off chance that you seriously love avocados and desire a fresh, brilliant treat, avocado squanders are the ideal tidbit or canapé. These squander consolidate the rich decency of ready avocados with a firm covering, making a great differentiation in surface. Here is a straightforward recipe to make these overwhelming avocado wastes.

Fixings:

2 ready avocados

1 cup regular baking flour

1 teaspoon baking powder

1/2 teaspoon garlic powder

1/2 teaspoon paprika

Salt and pepper to taste

1/2 cup milk

1 huge egg

1 cup breadcrumbs

Oil for broiling

Bearings:

Get ready Avocados: Strip and pit the avocados, then, at that point, cut them into reduced down lumps.

Blend Dry Fixings: In a bowl, consolidate the flour, baking powder, garlic powder, paprika, salt, and pepper.

Make Hitter: In another bowl, whisk together the milk and egg. Add the dry fixings to this combination, making a smooth hitter.

Coat Avocado Lumps: Dunk every avocado piece into the player, guaranteeing it's completely covered.

Breadcrumb Covering: Roll the player-covered avocado lumps in breadcrumbs, guaranteeing an even and liberal covering.

Heat Oil: In a profound skillet, heat oil for searing over medium-high intensity.

Sear Until Brilliant: Cautiously place the covered avocado lumps into the hot oil. Sear until they become brilliant brown, it are equitably cooked to guarantee all sides.

Channel Overabundance Oil: Once seared, utilize an opened spoon to move the wastes to a plate fixed with paper towels to deplete overabundance oil.

Serve Right away: Avocado squanders are best appreciated warm. Serve them with a plunging sauce of your decision, like salsa or garlic aioli.

Sustenance Data:

Serving Size: 4 wastes

Calories: Roughly 250 kcal

Protein: 6g

Starches: 30g

Fat: 12g

Fiber: 5g

Planning Time: 15 minutes

Cooking Time: 10 minutes

Servings: 4

These avocado squanders are a brilliant mix of fresh and smooth surfaces, making them a group-satisfying nibble for any event. Partake in the decency of avocados in a previously unheard-of manner with this simple-to-follow recipe!

Spinach and Artichoke Plunge

Fixings:

1 (10-ounce) bundle of frozen hacked spinach, defrosted and depleted

1 (14-ounce) can artichoke hearts, depleted and hacked

1/2 cup mayonnaise

1/2 cup harsh cream

1 cup ground Parmesan cheddar

1 cup destroyed mozzarella cheddar

1 teaspoon minced garlic

Salt and pepper to taste

1/4 teaspoon squashed red pepper chips (discretionary)

Bearings:

Preheat your stove to 375°F (190°C).

In a blending bowl, join the depleted spinach, slashed artichoke hearts, mayonnaise, harsh cream, ground Parmesan cheddar, destroyed mozzarella cheddar, minced garlic, salt, and pepper. Add squashed red pepper pieces for a smidgen of zest, whenever wanted.

Blend every one of the fixings until all around consolidated, guaranteeing an even dispersion of flavors.

Move the combination to a baking dish, spreading it out uniformly.

Prepare in the preheated stove for 25-30 minutes or until the plunge is hot and effervescent, and the top is brilliant brown.

Eliminate from the stove and let it cool for a couple of moments before serving.

Planning Time: 15 minutes

Cooking Time: 25-30 minutes

Serving: Around 8 servings

Sustenance Data (per serving):

Calories: 220

All out Fat: 18g

Immersed Fat: 7g

Cholesterol: 30mg

Sodium: 450mg

All out Sugars: 5g

Dietary Fiber: 2g

Sugars: 1g

Protein: 8g

Bison Cauliflower Nibbles

Fixings:

1 head of cauliflower, cut into reduced down florets

1 cup of regular baking flour

1 cup of water

1 teaspoon garlic powder

1 teaspoon onion powder

1/2 teaspoon salt

1/4 teaspoon dark pepper

1 cup hot sauce

2 tablespoons liquefied spread

Discretionary: celery sticks and farm dressing for serving

Planning Time: 15 minutes

Cooking Time: 25 minutes

Servings: 4

Nourishment Data (per serving):

Calories: 180

Fat: 5g

Starches: 30g

Fiber: 5g

Protein: 7g

Bearings:

Preheat your stove to 450°F (230°C) and line a baking sheet with material paper.

In a bowl, whisk together the flour, water, garlic powder, onion powder, salt, and dark pepper to make a smooth hitter.

Plunge every cauliflower floret into the player, guaranteeing it's very much covered, and put it on the pre-arranged baking sheet.

Heat the cauliflower in the preheated broiler for 20 minutes or until brilliant brown, flipping part of the way through for even firmness.

While the cauliflower is heating up, blend the hot sauce and liquefied spread in a different bowl.

When the cauliflower is finished, cautiously throw the heated florets in the hot sauce combination until uniformly covered.

Return the covered cauliflower to the baking sheet and prepare for 5 extra minutes to permit the sauce to set.

Eliminate from the stove, and let the bison cauliflower nibbles cool for a couple of moments.

Serve the nibbles on a platter with celery sticks as an afterthought and a bowl of farm dressing for plunging.

Chapter 3: Low Carb Main Dishes.

Fixings:

4 boneless, skinless chicken bosoms

1 tablespoon olive oil

1 teaspoon garlic powder

1 teaspoon paprika

Salt and pepper to taste

1 cup broccoli florets

1 cup cherry tomatoes, split

1/2 cup ground Parmesan cheddar

Bearings:

Planning Time (15 minutes):

Preheat your stove to 400°F (200°C).

Season the chicken bosoms with garlic powder, paprika, salt, and pepper.

Cut the broccoli into little florets and split the cherry tomatoes.

Cooking Time (25 minutes):

In a broiler-safe skillet, heat olive oil over medium-high intensity.

Burn the chicken bosoms for 3-4 minutes on each side until brilliant brown.

Add broccoli and cherry tomatoes to the skillet.

Move the skillet to the preheated broiler and prepare for 20 minutes or until the chicken arrives at an inside temperature of 165°F (74°C).

Serving (4 servings):

Plate the chicken bosoms with a liberal serving of the simmered vegetables.

Sprinkle Parmesan cheddar over the top for an additional eruption of flavor.

Sustenance Data (per serving):

Calories: 350

Protein: 40g

Sugars: 8g

Fiber: 3g

Sugars: 3g

Fat: 18g

Immersed Fat: 5g

Cholesterol: 110mg

Sodium: 400mg

Why this dish is a victor:

Low Carb: With just 8g of carbs per serving, this dish squeezes well into a low-carb way of life.

High Protein: Loaded with 40g of protein, it's incredible for muscle upkeep and feeling satisfied.

Supplement Rich Veggies: Broccoli and tomatoes bring nutrients, minerals, and fiber to the plate.

Fast and Simple: With a planning season of 15 minutes and a cooking season of 25 minutes, this recipe is ideal for occupied nights.

Lemon Spice Salmon

Fixings:

4 salmon filets

2 lemons (zested and squeezed)

2 tablespoons olive oil

2 cloves garlic (minced)

1 teaspoon dried thyme

1 teaspoon dried rosemary

Salt and pepper to taste

New parsley for decorating

Headings:

Preheat the Broiler: Preheat your stove to 375°F (190°C).

Set up the Marinade: In a little bowl, combine as one the lemon zing, lemon juice, olive oil, minced garlic, dried thyme, dried rosemary, salt, and pepper. This makes a tasty marinade for the salmon.

Marinate the Salmon: Spot the salmon filets in a shallow dish and pour the marinade over them. Guarantee that each filet is all around covered.

Permit the salmon to marinate for something like 15-20 minutes to assimilate the flavors.

Heat the Salmon: Move the marinated salmon filets to a baking dish fixed with material paper. Heat in the preheated broiler for roughly 15-20 minutes or until the salmon is cooked through and effectively drops with a fork.

Enhancement and Serve: When the salmon is finished, decorate it with new parsley for an eruption of variety and added newness. Serve the Lemon Spice Salmon with your #1 sides, like steamed vegetables or a light plate of mixed greens.

Sustenance Data (Per Serving):

Calories: Around 300 kcal

Protein: 25g

Fat: 20g

Starches: 3g

Fiber: 1g

Sugars: 1g

Sodium: Shifts because of added salt

Planning Time: 15 minutes

Cooking Time: 15-20 minutes

Servings: 4

Partake in this Lemon Spice Salmon for a magnificent feast that joins the extravagance of salmon with the splendor of lemon and the flavorful notes of spices. It's a fast and simple recipe that is certain to turn into a number one in your collection.

Chicken Parmesan Pieces

Planning Time: 15 minutes

Cooking Time: 15 minutes

Servings: 4

Fixings:

1 pound boneless, skinless chicken bosoms, cut into scaled-down pieces

1 cup breadcrumbs

1/2 cup ground Parmesan cheddar

1 teaspoon dried oregano

1 teaspoon dried basil

1/2 teaspoon garlic powder

Salt and pepper to taste

2 eggs, beaten

1 cup marinara sauce

1 cup destroyed mozzarella cheddar

New basil leaves for decorating

Headings:

Preheat your broiler to 400°F (200°C) and line a baking sheet with material paper.

In a bowl, join breadcrumbs, ground Parmesan, dried oregano, dried basil, garlic powder, salt, and pepper. Blend well to make the covering combination.

Dunk every chicken piece into the beaten eggs, they are completely covered to guarantee they.

Roll the egg-covered chicken pieces in the breadcrumb blend, squeezing delicately to ensure the covering sticks.

Put the covered chicken tenders on the pre-arranged baking sheet, guaranteeing they are dispersed equitably.

Prepare in the preheated broiler for around 12-15 minutes or until the pieces are brilliant brown and cooked through.

As of now baking, spoon a spot of marinara sauce onto every piece and sprinkle with destroyed mozzarella cheddar.

Return the baking sheet to the stove and prepare until the cheddar is liquefied and effervescent.

Once finished, eliminate from the broiler and let the pieces cool for a couple of moments.

Embellish with new basil leaves and serve hot with extra marinara sauce as an afterthought for plunging.

Sustenance Data (per serving):

Note: Sustenance values might shift given explicit fixings utilized.

Calories: 350

Protein: 30g

Carbs: 20g

Fat: 15g

Fiber: 2g

Sugars: 3g

Bacon-Wrapped Asparagus Packs

Fixings:

1 pack of new asparagus lances

8-10 cuts of bacon

Olive oil

Salt and pepper to taste

Planning Time:

Roughly 15 minutes

Cooking Time:

20-25 minutes

Servings:

4

Nourishment Data (per serving):

Calories: 180

Protein: 10g

Fat: 14g

Starches: 5g

Fiber: 3g

Bearings:

Preheat the Stove:

Preheat your stove to 400°F (200°C).

Set up the Asparagus:

Trim the extreme closures of the asparagus lances and sprinkle them with olive oil. Season with salt and pepper.

Wrap with Bacon:

Take 4-5 asparagus lances and pack them together. Fold a cut of bacon over each group, guaranteeing it holds the asparagus firmly.

Secure with Toothpicks:

Use toothpicks to get the bacon set up. This step guarantees that the bacon stays wrapped during cooking.

Orchestrate on a Baking Sheet:

Put the packs on a baking sheet, they are equitably dispersed to guarantee they. This takes into account in any event, cooking.

Heat Flawlessly:

Place the baking sheet in the preheated broiler and heat for 20-25 minutes or until the bacon becomes fresh.

Serve and Appreciate:

Once cooked, eliminate the toothpicks and move the packs to a serving plate. These Bacon-Wrapped Asparagus Packs are prepared to dazzle!

Barbecued Chicken Bosom with Lemon Spice Sauce

Planning Time: 15 minutes

Cooking Time: 15 minutes

Servings: 4

Fixings:

4 boneless, skinless chicken bosoms

2 tablespoons olive oil

2 teaspoons dried oregano

2 teaspoons dried thyme

Salt and pepper to taste

For Lemon Spice Sauce:

1/4 cup new lemon juice

2 tablespoons cleaved new parsley

1 tablespoon cleaved new basil

2 cloves garlic, minced

1/4 cup additional virgin olive oil

Salt and pepper to taste

Bearings:

Preheat the Barbecue:

Preheat your barbecue to medium-high intensity.

Get ready Chicken:

In a little bowl, blend olive oil, dried oregano, dried thyme, salt, and pepper.

Rub the chicken bosoms with this blend, it are very much covered to guarantee they.

Barbecue Chicken:

Put the chicken bosoms on the preheated barbecue.

Barbecue for roughly 6-8 minutes for every side or until the interior temperature comes to 165°F (74°C).

Plan Lemon Spice Sauce:

In a different bowl, whisk together lemon juice, slashed parsley, cleaved basil, minced garlic, additional virgin olive oil, salt, and pepper.

Serve:

When the chicken is completely cooked, move it to a serving plate.

Sprinkle the lemon spice sauce over the barbecued chicken bosoms.

Sustenance Data (per serving):

Calories: 300

Protein: 30g

Fat: 18g

Sugars: 2g

Fiber: 1g

Sugar: 0g

Sodium: 400mg

Zucchini Noodles with Pesto and Cherry Tomatoes

Fixings:

4 medium-sized zucchinis

1 cup cherry tomatoes, divided

1/2 cup pine nuts

2 cups new basil leaves

1/2 cup ground Parmesan cheddar

2 cloves garlic, minced

1/2 cup extra-virgin olive oil

Salt and pepper to taste

Headings:

Set up the Zucchini Noodles:

Utilizing a spiralizer or a vegetable peeler, make zucchini noodles.

Sprinkle the noodles with salt and allow them to sit for 15 minutes to deliver an abundance of dampness.

Wipe the noodles off with a paper towel to eliminate the dampness.

Make the Pesto:

In a food processor, join basil, pine nuts, Parmesan cheddar, garlic, salt, and pepper.

Beat the fixings until coarsely slashed.

With the processor running, gradually add the olive oil until the pesto arrives at a smooth consistency.

Sauté Zucchini Noodles:

Heat an enormous skillet over medium intensity.

Add a tablespoon of olive oil and sauté the zucchini noodles for 2-3 minutes until they are simply delicate yet at the same time have a slight crunch.

Consolidate and Throw:

In a similar dish, add the divided cherry tomatoes to the zucchini noodles.

Mix in the newly pre-arranged pesto, it is equitably covered to guarantee the noodles.

Cook for 2 extra minutes, permitting the flavors to merge.

Serve:

Plate the zucchini noodles with pesto and cherry tomatoes.

Alternatively, decorate with additional Parmesan cheddar and a sprinkle of pine nuts.

Sustenance Data (Per Serving):

Calories: 300

Protein: 8g

Sugars: 10g

Fiber: 4g

Fat: 25g

Immersed Fat: 4g

Cholesterol: 8mg

Sodium: 150mg

Planning Time: 20 minutes

Cooking Time: 10 minutes

Servings: 4

Heated Salmon with Garlic Spread

Planning Time: 15 minutes

Cooking Time: 20 minutes

Servings: 4

Fixings:

4 salmon filets

4 tablespoons unsalted margarine, liquefied

4 cloves garlic, minced

2 tablespoons new lemon juice

1 teaspoon dried oregano

1 teaspoon paprika

Salt and dark pepper to taste

New parsley, cleaved (for decorating)

Sustenance Data (per serving):

Calories: 300

Protein: 25g

Fat: 20g

Sugars: 2g

Fiber: 0.5g

Headings:

Preheat Broiler: Preheat your stove to 375°F (190°C).

Plan Salmon: Wipe the salmon filets off with paper towels. Put them on a baking sheet fixed with material paper.

Make Garlic Spread: In a little bowl, blend the softened margarine, minced garlic, lemon juice, oregano, paprika, salt, and pepper. Mix until all around consolidated.

Coat Salmon: Brush the garlic spread blend liberally over every salmon filet, guaranteeing an in any event, covering.

Heat: Spot the baking sheet in the preheated broiler and prepare for roughly 15-20 minutes or until the salmon chips effectively with a fork. The cooking time might shift given the thickness of your filets.

Decorate: Once heated, eliminate the salmon from the broiler and topping with newly hacked parsley.

Serve: Serve the heated salmon hot, matched with your number one sides like steamed vegetables or an invigorating plate of mixed greens.

Sustenance Tip: Salmon is rich in omega-3 unsaturated fats, which are helpful for heart wellbeing. Furthermore, garlic gives an increase in flavor while offering potential medical advantages, including resistant framework support.

Cauliflower Broiled Rice with Shrimp

Planning Time: 15 minutes

Cooking Time: 15 minutes

Serving: 4

Sustenance Data (per serving):

Calories: 250

Protein: 20g

Fat: 12g

Starches: 15g

Fiber: 7g

Fixings:

1 medium-sized cauliflower, ground

1 pound shrimp, stripped and deveined

2 eggs, beaten

1 cup blended vegetables (peas, carrots, corn)

4 green onions, finely slashed

3 cloves garlic, minced

2 tablespoons soy sauce

1 tablespoon sesame oil

1 tablespoon olive oil

Salt and pepper to taste

Bearings:

Set up the Cauliflower Rice:

Grind the cauliflower utilizing a case grater or a food processor until it looks like rice grains.

Steam or microwave the cauliflower rice for around 5 minutes until it becomes delicate. Put away.

Cook the Shrimp:

In a huge skillet, heat olive oil over medium intensity.

Add minced garlic and sauté until fragrant.

Add shrimp to the skillet and cook until they become pink and hazy, generally 2-3 minutes for each side. Eliminate shrimp and put it away.

Vegetable Variety:

In a similar skillet, add blended vegetables and cook until they are delicate yet still fresh.

Push the vegetables aside from the skillet and empty the beaten eggs into the opposite side.

Scramble the eggs until completely cooked, then blend them in with the vegetables.

Consolidate Fixings:

Add the cauliflower rice to the skillet, mixing great to join with the vegetables and eggs.

Delightful Completion:

Pour soy sauce and sesame oil over the combination, guaranteeing even the conveyance of flavors.

Season with salt and pepper as indicated by taste.

Unite Everything:

Tenderly overlay in the cooked shrimp and slashed green onions, permitting them to mix with the cauliflower rice.

Serve and Appreciate:

Dole out the Cauliflower Seared Rice with Shrimp onto plates and trim with extra green onions whenever you want.

Chapter 4: Vegetarian Keto Delights

Fixings:

Cauliflower rice

Avocado

Zucchini

Olive oil

Spinach

Broccoli

Coconut oil

Almonds

Tofu

Garlic

Salt and pepper

Healthful yeast

Planning Time:

20 minutes

Cooking Time:

30 minutes

Servings:

4

Nourishment Data (per serving):

Calories: 300

Fat: 25g

Carbs: 10g

Fiber: 5g

Protein: 12g

Bearings:

Get ready for Cauliflower Rice:

Grind cauliflower into rice-sized pieces.

Sauté in olive oil until delicate.

Avocado Crush:

Crush avocado with salt and pepper.

Zucchini Noodles:

Spiralize zucchini into noodles.

Sauté in coconut oil until still somewhat firm.

Sauteed Greens:

Sauté spinach, broccoli, and garlic in olive oil until withered.

Tofu Crunch:

3D square tofu and sear until brilliant.

Smash almonds and blend in with wholesome yeast for covering.

Roll tofu in the blend for a crunchy surface.

Gathering:

Place cauliflower rice as the base.

Add zucchini noodles, sautéed greens, and avocado squash.

Top with crunchy tofu.

Serve and Appreciate:

Embellish with a shower of olive oil and a sprinkle of salt and pepper.

Plunge into a fantastic, low-carb, veggie-lover keto feast.

Eggplant Pizzas

Fixings:

2 huge eggplants

1 cup marinara sauce

1 cup destroyed mozzarella cheddar

1/4 cup ground Parmesan cheddar

1 teaspoon dried oregano

1 teaspoon dried basil

Salt and pepper to taste

Olive oil for brushing

Planning Time:

15 minutes

Cooking Time:

20 minutes

Servings:

4

Sustenance Data:

(Per serving)

Calories: 180

Protein: 9g

Sugars: 15g

Fiber: 7g

Fat: 10g

Immersed Fat: 4.5g

Cholesterol: 20mg

Sodium: 450mg

Headings:

Preheat the Broiler:

Set your broiler to 400°F (200°C).

Set up the Eggplant:

Wash and trim the closures of the eggplants.

Cut them into 1/2-inch thick adjusts.

Season the Eggplant:

Put eggplant adjusts on a baking sheet.

Brush each side with olive oil and sprinkle with salt and pepper.

Prepare the Eggplant:

Prepare the eggplant adjusts for 10-12 minutes until they become delicate.

Top with Sauce and Cheddar:

Eliminate the eggplants from the broiler.

Spoon marinara sauce onto each round, then, at that point, sprinkle with mozzarella and Parmesan cheddar.

Add Flavors:

Sprinkle dried oregano and basil over the top for added character.

Get back to the Broiler:

Set the beat eggplants back in the stove and heat for an extra 8-10 minutes or until the cheddar is softened and effervescent.

Serve and Appreciate:

Permit the eggplant pizzas to cool for a couple of moments before serving.

Decorate with new basil whenever you want.

Portobello Mushroom Burgers

Planning Time: 15 minutes

Cooking Time: 15 minutes

Servings: 4 burgers

Fixings:

4 enormous Portobello mushrooms

1/4 cup balsamic vinegar

2 tablespoons olive oil

2 cloves garlic, minced

1 teaspoon dried oregano

Salt and pepper to taste

4 entire grain burger buns

Fixings: lettuce, tomato, red onion, and your number-one sauces

Bearings:

Clean and Marinate:

Tenderly perfect the Portobello mushrooms with a clammy material. Eliminate stems.

In a bowl, blend balsamic vinegar, olive oil, minced garlic, dried oregano, salt, and pepper to make a marinade.

Marinate Mushrooms:

Place mushrooms in a shallow dish, gill side up.

Brush the marinade over each mushroom, guaranteeing an in any event, covering.

Allow them to marinate for somewhere around 10 minutes, permitting flavors to be injected.

Preheat Barbecue:

Preheat your barbecue or barbecue skillet to medium-high intensity.

Barbecue Mushrooms:

Put marinated mushrooms on the barbecue, gill side down.

Barbecue for around 5-7 minutes on each side, or until delicate and succulent.

Toast Buns:

As of now of barbecuing, put the entire grain buns on the barbecue to toast delicately.

Gather Burgers:

Put barbecued Portobello mushrooms on the toasted buns.

Add your number one garnish: lettuce, tomato cuts, red onion, and any favored sauces.

Serve and Appreciate:

Serve your Portobello Mushroom Burgers quickly while they're hot.

Sustenance Data (per serving):

Calories: 250

Protein: 8g

Starches: 30g

Fat: 12g

Fiber: 5g

Cauliflower Bison Nibbles

Fixings:

1 head of cauliflower, cut into reduced down florets

1 cup regular baking flour

1 cup water

1 teaspoon garlic powder

1 teaspoon onion powder

1/2 teaspoon salt

1/4 teaspoon dark pepper

1 cup hot sauce

2 tablespoons liquefied margarine

Green onions, cleaved (for decorating)

Planning Time: 15 minutes

Cooking Time: 25 minutes

Servings: 4

Nourishment Data (per serving):

Calories: 200

Protein: 5g

Starches: 30g

Fiber: 4g

Fat: 8g

Soaked Fat: 4g

Cholesterol: 15mg

Sodium: 1200mg

Bearings:

Preheat Stove: Preheat your broiler to 450°F (230°C) and line a baking sheet with material paper.

Get ready Cauliflower: Cut the cauliflower into reduced down florets, guaranteeing they are comparative in size for cooking.

Make Hitter: In a bowl, whisk together the flour, water, garlic powder, onion powder, salt, and dark pepper until you have a smooth player.

Coat Cauliflower: Dunk every cauliflower floret into the hitter, it is equally covered to guarantee it. Shake off the abundance hitter and put the covered florets on the pre-arranged baking sheet.

Prepare: Heat in the preheated stove for 20-25 minutes or until the cauliflower is brilliant and fresh, turning it partially through for cooking.

Get ready Hot Sauce: While the cauliflower is heating up, combine the hot sauce and dissolved margarine in a bowl.

Cover with Hot Sauce: When the cauliflower is finished, move it to a huge bowl and pour the hot sauce blend over it. Tenderly throw until the cauliflower is completely covered.

Serve: Orchestrate the cauliflower nibbles on a serving platter and trim with cleaved green onions.

Avocado Serving of mixed greens

Fixings:

3 ready avocados, diced

1 cup cherry tomatoes, divided

1 cucumber, diced

1/2 red onion, finely slashed

1/4 cup new cilantro, slashed

1 lime, squeezed

2 tablespoons olive oil

Salt and pepper to taste

Planning Time: 15 minutes

Cooking Time: 0 minutes

Servings: 4

Nourishment Data (per serving):

Calories: 220

Fat: 18g

Carbs: 14g

Fiber: 8g

Protein: 3g

Bearings:

Get ready for Vegetables:

Dice the avocados, split the cherry tomatoes, and cleave the cucumber, red onion, and cilantro.

Consolidate Fixings:

In a huge blending bowl, delicately consolidate the diced avocados, cherry tomatoes, cucumber, red onion, and cilantro.

Make Dressing:

In a little bowl, whisk together the lime juice, olive oil, salt, and pepper to make a lively dressing.

Throw and Coat:

Pour the dressing over the avocado blend and delicately throw until all fixings are equitably covered.

Serve Right away:

Serve the avocado plate of mixed greens quickly to keep up with its newness and dynamic tones.

Tips:

Pick ready avocados for a rich surface.

Redo with your number one vegetable or add a protein like barbecued chicken or shrimp.

Change lime, salt, and pepper to suit your taste inclinations.

Zucchini Noodles with Pesto

Fixings:

4 medium-sized zucchinis

2 cups new basil leaves

1/2 cup ground Parmesan cheddar

1/2 cup pine nuts

2 garlic cloves

1/2 cup extra-virgin olive oil

Salt and pepper to taste

Planning Time: 15 minutes

Cooking Time: 5 minutes

Servings: 4

Nourishment Data (per serving):

Calories: 250

Protein: 5g

Starches: 8g

Fat: 23g

Fiber: 3g

Bearings:

Set up the Zucchini Noodles:

Utilizing a spiralizer, make zucchini noodles by spiralizing the zucchini. If you don't have a spiralizer, a vegetable peeler can be utilized to make dainty strips look like noodles.

Make the Pesto Sauce:

In a food processor, consolidate basil, Parmesan cheddar, pine nuts, garlic cloves, salt, and pepper.

While handling, slowly add the olive oil until a smooth pesto sauce is framed.

Cook the Zucchini Noodles:

Heat a huge skillet over medium intensity.

Add the zucchini noodles to the skillet and sauté for around 3-5 minutes until they are delicate yet have a slight crunch.

Join and Serve:

Pour the pre-arranged pesto sauce over the cooked zucchini noodles.

Throw the noodles until they are very much covered with the pesto.

Serve right away, alternatively decorating with extra Parmesan cheddar and pine nuts.

Appreciate:

Enjoy a light, delightful, and solid dish that is rich in supplements and low in carbs.

Cauliflower Crust Pizza

Cauliflower Outside Pizza

Fixings:

1 medium-sized cauliflower

1 egg

1 cup destroyed mozzarella cheddar

1 teaspoon dried oregano

1/2 teaspoon garlic powder

Salt and pepper to taste

Pizza sauce

Your #1 pizza garnishes (e.g., tomatoes, olives, mushrooms, spinach)

Planning Time: 20 minutes

Cooking Time: 25 minutes

Servings: 2-4 (contingent upon size)

Nourishment Data (per serving):

Calories: Roughly 150 kcal

Protein: 10g

Sugars: 10g

Fat: 8g

Fiber: 5g

Bearings:

Preheat the Stove:

Preheat your stove to 400°F (200°C). Place a pizza stone or a baking sheet on the stove to warm.

Set up the Cauliflower:

Cut the cauliflower into florets and heartbeat in a food processor until it looks like rice.

Cook the Cauliflower:

Microwave the riced cauliflower for 5-6 minutes or until delicate. Permit it to cool.

Channel Overabundance Dampness:

Move the cooked cauliflower to a perfect kitchen towel and press out however much dampness as could reasonably be expected.

Blend Fixings:

In a bowl, join the cauliflower, egg, destroyed mozzarella, oregano, garlic powder, salt, and pepper. Blend until a mixture structure.

Shape the Covering:

Put the cauliflower combination on a material paper-lined surface and shape it into a pizza hull of your ideal thickness.

Heat the Covering:

Move the outside layer (with material paper) onto the preheated pizza stone or baking sheet. Heat for 15-18 minutes or until the covering is brilliant brown.

Add Garnishes:

Eliminate the outside layer from the stove and spread the pizza sauce uniformly. Add your number one garnishes.

Complete the process of Baking:

Return the pizza to the stove and heat for an extra 8-10 minutes or until the cheddar is dissolved and effervescent.

Serve and Appreciate:

Permit the pizza to cool for a couple of moments, then, at that point, cut and serve. Partake in your faultless, cauliflower outside-layer pizza!

Eggplant Lasagna

Planning Time: 30 minutes

Cooking Time: 45 minutes

Servings: 6-8

Fixings:

2 huge eggplants, meagerly cut

1 pound ground meat or Italian frankfurter (discretionary)

1 onion, finely hacked

3 cloves garlic, minced

1 can (28 ounces) squashed tomatoes

2 cups ricotta cheddar

1 cup ground Parmesan cheddar

2 cups destroyed mozzarella cheddar

1 teaspoon dried oregano

1 teaspoon dried basil

Salt and pepper to taste

Olive oil for sautéing

New basil for decorating (discretionary)

Sustenance Data (per serving):

Calories: 400

Protein: 25g

Sugars: 15g

Fat: 28g

Fiber: 5g

Headings:

Preheat the Broiler: Preheat your stove to 375°F (190°C).

Plan Eggplant Cuts: Lay the meagerly cut eggplant on a baking sheet, sprinkle with salt and allow it to sit for around 15 minutes. This helps draw out abundance dampness. Wipe the eggplant off with paper towels.

Sauté the Meat (Discretionary): In a skillet, cook the ground hamburger or Italian hotdog over medium intensity until seared. Eliminate overabundance of fat, if any.

Sauté Onions and Garlic: In a similar skillet, sauté the hacked onion and minced garlic in olive oil until relaxed.

Add Tomatoes: Pour in the squashed tomatoes, dried oregano, dried basil, salt, and pepper. Stew for 15-20 minutes, permitting the flavors to merge.

Get ready Cheddar Blend: In a bowl, combine one ricotta cheddar, a big part of the Parmesan cheddar, and a big part of the destroyed mozzarella.

Collect the Lasagna: In a lubed baking dish, layer the eggplant cuts, meat (if utilizing), pureed tomatoes, and cheddar combination. Rehash until all fixings are utilized, wrapping up with a layer of cheddar on top.

Prepare: Cover the dish with foil and heat for 30 minutes. Uncover and sprinkle the excess Parmesan and mozzarella cheddar on top. Heat for 15 extra minutes or until the cheddar is brilliant and effervescent.

Serve: Permit the eggplant lasagna to rest for a couple of moments before serving. Embellish with new basil whenever you want.

Chapter 5: side dishes

Fixings:

2 cups of your #1 vegetables (broccoli, carrots, and chime peppers function admirably)

3 tablespoons olive oil

2 cloves garlic, minced

1 teaspoon dried spices (rosemary or thyme)

Salt and pepper to taste

Planning Time: 10 minutes

Cooking Time: 20 minutes

Serving: 4

Bearings:

Preheat the Stove: Preheat your broiler to 400°F (200°C).

Get ready Vegetables: Wash and cleave the vegetables into scaled-down pieces.

Preparing: In a bowl, blend the vegetables with olive oil, minced garlic, dried spices, salt, and pepper. Guarantee an in any event, covering.

Baking: Spread the carefully prepared vegetables on a baking sheet in a solitary layer. Heat for around 20 minutes or until they are brilliant and delicate.

Serve: Once cooked, move the vegetables to a serving dish. Sprinkle extra spices for a new touch.

Nourishment Data:

This side dish isn't just delightful but also nutritious. It gives a decent wellspring of fiber, nutrients, and sound fats. The olive oil adds a portion of heart-sound monounsaturated fats, while the different vegetables offer a scope of fundamental supplements.

Calories: Around 120 for each serving

Fat: 9g

Sugars: 10g

Fiber: 3g

Protein: 2g

Tips:

Explore different avenues regarding various spices and flavors to modify the flavor profile.

Add a press of lemon juice or a sprinkle of Parmesan cheddar for an additional eruption of flavor.

Go ahead and blend and match vegetables in light of your inclinations or occasional accessibility.

Messy Broccoli Nibbles

Fixings:

2 cups broccoli florets, finely slashed

1 cup cheddar, destroyed

1/2 cup breadcrumbs

1/4 cup Parmesan cheddar, ground

2 enormous eggs

2 cloves garlic, minced

1/2 teaspoon onion powder

Salt and pepper to taste

Cooking splash

Planning Time: 15 minutes

Cooking Time: 20 minutes

Servings: Roughly 20 chomps

Nourishment Data (per serving):

Calories: 70

Protein: 4g

Sugars: 5g

Fat: 4g

Fiber: 1g

Headings:

Preheat your broiler to 375°F (190°C) and line a baking sheet with material paper. Gently cover it with a cooking shower to forestall staying.

Steam the broccoli florets until they are delicate yet at the same time firm, for around 3-4 minutes. Permit them to marginally cool.

In an enormous blending bowl, join the slashed broccoli, cheddar, breadcrumbs, Parmesan cheddar, minced garlic, onion powder, salt, and pepper. Blend well to guarantee even dissemination of fixings.

Beat the eggs in a different bowl and afterward add them to the broccoli blend. Mix until everything is very much joined and starts to remain together.

With clean hands, shape the blend into scaled-down balls and put them on the pre-arranged baking sheet, they are uniformly divided to guarantee they.

Prepare in the preheated stove for 15-20 minutes or until the chomps become brilliant brown and fresh outward.

Permit the Messy Broccoli Chomps to cool for a couple of moments before serving.

Garlic Parmesan Brussels Fledglings

Planning Time: 15 minutes

Cooking Time: 25 minutes

Servings: 4

Fixings:

1 pound Brussels grows, managed, and split

3 tablespoons olive oil

3 cloves garlic, minced

1/2 cup ground Parmesan cheddar

Salt and pepper to taste

1 tablespoon balsamic vinegar (discretionary)

Cleaved new parsley for embellish

Bearings:

Preheat the Stove: Preheat your broiler to 400°F (200°C).

Get ready Brussels Fledglings: Trim the closures of the Brussels fledglings and cut them down the middle. Place them in an enormous bowl.

Add Garlic and Olive Oil: In a little bowl, blend minced garlic with olive oil. Pour the combination over the Brussels fledglings and throw until all around is covered.

Preparing: Sprinkle the Brussels sprouts with salt and pepper as indicated by your taste. Throw again to disseminate the flavoring uniformly.

Broiling: Spread the Brussels grows uniformly on a baking sheet. Cook on the preheated stove for around 20-25 minutes or until they are brilliant brown and fresh on the edges.

Parmesan Besting: During the most recent 5 minutes of broiling, sprinkle the ground Parmesan cheddar over the Brussels sprouts. This will dissolve and make a flavorful, messy hull.

Discretionary Balsamic Coating: Whenever wanted, sprinkle balsamic vinegar over the simmered Brussels sprouts for a tart kick.

Embellish: When out of the broiler, decorate with hacked new parsley for an explosion of variety and added newness.

Serve: Move the Garlic Parmesan Brussels Fledglings to a serving dish and serve right away.

Sustenance Data (per serving):

Calories: 180

All out Fat: 12g

Immersed Fat: 3g

Cholesterol: 10mg

Sodium: 180mg

All out Sugars: 15g

Dietary Fiber: 6g

Sugars: 3g

Protein: 8g

Rosemary Jicama Fries

Fixings:

1 huge jicama, stripped and cut into flimsy strips

2 tablespoons olive oil

1 tablespoon new rosemary, hacked

1 teaspoon garlic powder

Salt and pepper to taste

Planning Time: 15 minutes

Cooking Time: 25 minutes

Servings: 4

Nourishment Data (per serving):

Calories: 120

Fat: 7g

Carbs: 15g

Fiber: 11g

Protein: 1g

Bearings:

Preheat the Stove: Preheat your broiler to 400°F (200°C).

Get ready Jicama: Strip the jicama and cut it into slight strips that look like conventional fries.

Preparing Blend: In a bowl, consolidate olive oil, cleaved rosemary, garlic powder, salt, and pepper. Blend well.

Coat the Chips: Throw the jicama fries in the flavoring blend until they are uniformly covered.

Orchestrate on Baking Sheet: Put the carefully prepared jicama fries on a baking sheet in a solitary layer, they are not packed to guarantee they. This guarantees in any event, cooking and firmness.

Prepare: Heat in the preheated broiler for roughly 20-25 minutes or until the French fries are brilliant brown and firm. Flip the chips partially through the cooking time for even freshness.

Serve: Once finished, eliminate them from the stove and let them cool for a couple of moments. Serve the rosemary jicama fries with your most loved plunging sauce.

Nourishment Tips:

Jicama is low in calories and high in fiber, making it a sound option in contrast to customary fries.

Olive oil adds sound fats and a rich flavor profile.

Rosemary improves the taste as well as gives cell reinforcements.

Simmered Garlic Pureed potatoes

Nutrition Data:

Calories: 220 for every serving

Fat: 8g

Sugars: 35g

Protein: 4g

Fixings:

2 lbs (around 4 enormous) chestnut potatoes, stripped and diced

1 head of garlic

1 cup entire milk

1/2 cup unsalted spread

Salt and pepper to taste

Slashed new chives for embellish (discretionary)

Bearings:

Broil the Garlic:

Preheat your broiler to 400°F (200°C).

Remove the highest point of the garlic head to uncover the cloves.

Shower with olive oil, enclose by foil, and meal for around 30 minutes or until cloves are brilliant and delicate.

Cook the Potatoes:

Heat the stripped and diced potatoes in a huge pot of salted water until delicate (around 15-20 minutes).

Channel the potatoes completely.

Pound and Mix:

In a different pan, heat the milk and margarine until the spread is dissolved.

Crush the potatoes and add the cooked garlic cloves.

Progressively pour in the warm milk-spread blend while proceeding to pound until smooth and velvety.

Prepare with unmistakable expertise:

Season the pureed potatoes with salt and pepper to taste.

Change the consistency by adding more milk if necessary.

Serve and Enhancement:

Move the pureed potatoes to a serving dish.

Decorate with cleaved new chives for an eruption of variety and added flavor.

Appreciate:

Serve these Simmered Garlic Pureed potatoes close by your #1 fundamental course and relish the velvety goodness.

Barbecued Asparagus with Lemon Zing

Fixings:

1 pack of new asparagus

2 tablespoons olive oil

1 lemon (zested and squeezed)

Salt and pepper to taste

Planning Time: 10 minutes

Cooking Time: 10 minutes

Serving: 4

Sustenance Data (per serving):

Calories: 80

Protein: 3g

Sugars: 6g

Fiber: 3g

Fat: 6g

L-ascorbic acid: 20% DV

Folate: 15% DV

Headings:

Preheat the Barbecue: Intensity your barbecue to medium-high intensity.

Set up the Asparagus: Trim the intense finishes off the asparagus lances. Place them in a huge bowl and throw with olive oil, salt, and pepper.

Barbecue the Asparagus: Orchestrate the asparagus lances on the preheated barbecue.

Barbecue for 4-5 minutes, turning sometimes, until they are delicate and somewhat burned.

Lemon Zing Blend: In a little bowl, consolidate the lemon zing and juice. Blend well.

Final detail: When the asparagus is finished, move it to a serving platter. Shower the lemon zing combination over the barbecued asparagus.

Serve: Trimming with extra lemon zing whenever wanted. Serve right away, and partake in the lively kinds of barbecued asparagus with a fiery contort!

Quinoa Salad with Cherry Tomatoes and Feta

Fixings:

1 cup quinoa

2 cups cherry tomatoes, split

1/2 cup feta cheddar, disintegrated

1/4 cup red onion, finely hacked

1/4 cup new parsley, hacked

2 tablespoons olive oil

1 tablespoon lemon juice

Salt and pepper to taste

Planning Time:

15 minutes

Cooking Time:

15 minutes

Servings:

4

Sustenance Data:

(Per Serving)

Calories: 300

Protein: 10g

Sugars: 35g

Fiber: 5g

Fat: 14g

Soaked Fat: 4g

Cholesterol: 15mg

Sodium: 250mg

Bearings:

Wash Quinoa:

Wash the quinoa under cool water to eliminate any sharpness. Cook it as per bundle directions.

Plan Vegetables:

While the quinoa is cooking, divide the cherry tomatoes, slash the red onion, and finely hack the new parsley.

Cushion Quinoa:

Once the quinoa is cooked, cushion it with a fork and let it cool to room temperature.

Join Fixings:

In an enormous bowl, join the cooked quinoa, cherry tomatoes, red onion, and new parsley.

Add Feta Cheddar:

Delicately crease in the disintegrated feta cheddar, guaranteeing an even appropriation all through the serving of mixed greens.

Make Dressing:

In a little bowl, whisk together the olive oil and lemon juice. Season with salt and pepper to taste.

Dress the Serving of mixed greens:

Pour the dressing over the quinoa combination and throw everything together until very much covered.

Chill and Serve:

Refrigerate the serving of mixed greens for no less than 30 minutes to permit the flavors to merge. Serve chilled and appreciate!

Sautéed Spinach with Garlic and Olive Oil

Planning Time: 10 minutes

Cooking Time: 5 minutes

Serving: 4

Fixings:

1 lb new spinach, washed and managed

3 tbsp olive oil

4 cloves garlic, minced

Salt and pepper to taste

Discretionary: red pepper pieces for a sprinkle of flavor

Lemon wedges for decorate

Sustenance Data (per serving):

Calories: 80

All out Fat: 7g

Immersed Fat: 1g

Cholesterol: 0mg

Sodium: 150mg

All out Starches: 3g

Dietary Fiber: 2g

Sugars: 0g

Protein: 2g

Vitamin D: 0%

Calcium: 6%

Iron: 15%

Potassium: 15%

Bearings:

Set up the Spinach:

Wash the spinach completely and trim any extreme stems.

Mince Garlic:

Strip and finely mince the garlic cloves.

Heat Olive Oil:

In a huge skillet, heat olive oil over medium intensity.

Sauté Garlic:

Add minced garlic to the warmed oil and sauté until brilliant brown, mixing as often as possible.

Add Spinach:

Bit by bit add the pre-arranged spinach to the skillet, permitting it to shrivel. Use utensils to throw and cover the spinach in the garlic-imbued oil.

Season:

Season with salt, pepper, and red pepper pieces whenever wanted. Keep on cooking until the spinach is simply withered yet at the same time lively green.

Serve:

Move the sautéed spinach to a serving dish. Decorate with lemon wedges for a reviving touch.

Sustenance Note:

This dish is plentiful in iron, L-ascorbic acid, and fiber. It makes for a supplement thick side or can be served over entire grains for a healthy dinner.

Appreciate:

Serve the Sautéed Spinach with Garlic and Olive Oil as a tasty and nutritious backup to your number one principal dishes.

Chapter 6: Snacks and Finger Foods

Guacamole and Salsa Nachos

Fixings:

Tortilla chips

2 ready avocados

1 little onion, finely cleaved

1 tomato, diced

1/4 cup new cilantro, cleaved

1 lime, squeezed

Salt and pepper to taste

Headings:

Squash avocados in a bowl and blend in with slashed onion, diced tomato, cilantro, lime squeeze, salt, and pepper.

Spread tortilla chips on a serving platter.

Spoon the guacamole over the chips.

Present with your #1 salsa as an afterthought.

Planning Time: 15 minutes

Cooking Time: 0 minutes

Serving: 4

2. Prepared Yam Fries

Fixings:

2 huge yams, cut into fries

2 tablespoons olive oil

1 teaspoon paprika

1 teaspoon garlic powder

Salt and pepper to taste

Bearings:

Preheat stove to 425°F (220°C).

Throw yam fries with olive oil, paprika, garlic powder, salt, and pepper.

Spread fries in a solitary layer on a baking sheet.

Prepare for 20-25 minutes, turning once, until fresh.

Planning Time: 10 minutes

Cooking Time: 20-25 minutes

Serving: 4

3. Caprese Sticks

Fixings:

Cherry tomatoes

New mozzarella balls

New basil leaves

Balsamic coating

Bearings:

String a tomato, mozzarella ball, and basil leaf onto little sticks.

Orchestrate sticks on a serving platter.

Shower with a balsamic coating not long before serving.

Planning Time: 10 minutes

Cooking Time: 0 minutes

Serving: 6

Nourishment Data:

Guacamole and Salsa Nachos:

Calories: 180 for each serving

Fat: 12g

Carbs: 18g

Protein: 3g

Prepared Yam Fries:

Calories: 150 for each serving

Fat: 7g

Carbs: 20g

Protein: 2g

Caprese Sticks:

Calories: 70 for each serving

Fat: 5g

Carbs: 2g

Protein: 5g

Keto Cheddar Crisps

Fixings:

1 cup destroyed Parmesan cheddar

1 cup destroyed sharp cheddar

Discretionary: Spices and flavors for flavor, (for example, garlic powder, paprika, or dried spices)

Planning Time: 10 minutes

Cooking Time: 10 minutes

Servings: Roughly 4 servings

Nourishment Data (per serving):

Calories: 120

Fat: 10g

Protein: 7g

Starches: 1g

Fiber: 0g

Net Carbs: 1g

Bearings:

Preheat your stove to 400°F (200°C) and line a baking sheet with material paper.

In a bowl, combine as one the destroyed Parmesan and cheddar. Alternatively, add spices and flavors for additional character.

Spoon little hills of the cheddar blend onto the pre-arranged baking sheet, leaving space between each hill. Straighten each hill marginally with the rear of the spoon.

Prepare in the preheated broiler for around 8-10 minutes or until the edges of the cheddar crisps are brilliant brown and fresh.

Eliminate the baking sheet from the broiler and let the crisps cool for a couple of moments on the sheet. They will keep on firming up as they cool.

Cautiously move the cheddar crisps to a wire rack to totally cool.

Once cooled, the keto cheddar crisps are fit to be delighted in as a crunchy nibble or a tasty garnish for plates of mixed greens.

Tips:

Explore different avenues regarding different cheddar assortments for novel flavor profiles.

Watch the crisps intently while baking to forestall consumption, as broiler temperatures can shift.

Bison Cauliflower Nibbles

Bison Cauliflower Nibbles are a great wind on the exemplary chicken wing, offering a scrumptious and veggie lover elective. These hot, tart nibbles are ideal for parties, game evenings, or even a relaxed tidbit. How about we plunge into the basic moves toward preparing this group pleaser?

Fixings:

1 head of cauliflower, cut into reduced down florets

1 cup regular flour

1 cup water

1 teaspoon garlic powder

1 teaspoon onion powder

1/2 teaspoon smoked paprika

1/2 teaspoon salt

1/4 teaspoon dark pepper

1 cup hot sauce

2 tablespoons softened margarine

Headings:

Preheat the Broiler: Preheat your stove to 450°F (230°C). This guarantees a high temperature for the cauliflower to freshen up.

Set up the Hitter: In a bowl, whisk together the flour, water, garlic powder, onion powder, smoked paprika, salt, and dark pepper until you have a smooth player.

Coat the Cauliflower: Dunk every cauliflower floret into the player, guaranteeing it's completely covered. Shake off the overabundance of players to stay away from clusters.

Prepare Flawlessly: Put the covered cauliflower on a baking sheet fixed with material paper. Heat for 20-25 minutes or until the chomps are brilliant and fresh.

Hot Sauce Sorcery: While the cauliflower is heating up, blend the hot sauce and dissolved margarine in a bowl.

Throw and Coating: When the cauliflower is finished, move it to an enormous bowl. Pour the hot sauce combination over the heated cauliflower and throw until each piece is liberally covered.

Serve and Appreciate: Organize the Bison Cauliflower Chomps on a plate and present them with your most loved plunging sauce, like a farm or blue cheddar.

Extra Tips:

For an additional kick, add a smidgen of cayenne pepper to the player or the hot sauce.

Modify the zest level by changing how much hot sauce is indicated by your taste.

Nourishment Data:

(Note: Nourishment values might shift in light of explicit fixings and part measures. The qualities underneath are estimated.)

Serving Size: 1 cup

Calories: 150

Protein: 5g

Starches: 25g

Fat: 4g

Fiber: 3g

Cinnamon Almond Crisps

Fixings:

1 cup almonds, cut

1 cup regular flour

1/2 cup unsalted spread, mellowed

1/2 cup granulated sugar

1 teaspoon ground cinnamon

1/4 teaspoon salt

1 teaspoon vanilla concentrate

Planning Time: 15 minutes

Cooking Time: 15 minutes

Servings: Roughly 20 crisps

Nourishment Data (per serving):

Calories: 120

Complete Fat: 8g

Soaked Fat: 3.5g

Cholesterol: 15mg

Sodium: 30mg

Complete Starches: 10g

Dietary Fiber: 1g

Sugars: 4g

Protein: 2g

Bearings:

Preheat the Stove:

Preheat your stove to 350°F (175°C). Line a baking sheet with material paper.

Get ready Almonds:

Spread the cut almonds equally on the baking sheet and toast them on the preheated stove for around 5-7 minutes or until brilliant brown. Watch out for them to forestall consumption. When toasted, put away to cool.

Blend Dry Fixings:

In a medium-sized bowl, whisk together the regular baking flour, ground cinnamon, and salt.

Cream Margarine and Sugar:

In a different enormous bowl, cream together the mellowed margarine and granulated sugar until light and soft.

Join Wet and Dry Fixings:

Steadily add the flour blend to the creamed margarine and sugar. Mix until very much consolidated. Gather vanilla concentrate and blend until the mixture comes into a single unit.

Overlap in Almonds:

Delicately overlay the toasted cut almonds into the mixture, it are uniformly conveyed to guarantee they.

Shape the Mixture:

Partition the mixture down the middle and shape each piece into a log, roughly 1.5 crawls in measurement. Envelop the logs with saran wrap and refrigerate for no less than 60 minutes.

Prepare:

Preheat the stove to 375°F (190°C). Cut the chilled batter signs into 1/4-inch thick adjusts and put them on the pre-arranged baking sheet. Prepare for 10-12 minutes or until the edges are brilliant brown.

Cool and Appreciate:

Permit the crisps to cool on the baking sheet for a couple of moments before moving them to a wire rack to totally cool. Once cooled, enjoy these Cinnamon Almond Crisps with your number one drink.

Cheese and Crackers

Arranged cheeses (Cheddar, Gouda, Brie, and so forth.)

Different wafers (entire wheat, water saltines, or your #1 decision)

Discretionary: Grapes, nuts, or honey for embellish

Planning Time:

10 minutes

Cooking Time:

None (gathering as it were)

Serving:

Ideal for 4-6 individuals as a tidbit or canapé.

Sustenance Data:

(Per serving)

Calories: Around 250 kcal

Protein: 10g

Fat: 18g

Sugars: 15g

Fiber: 2g

Headings:

Cheddar Determination:

Start by picking different cheeses to make an assorted flavor profile. Settle on a blend of hard and delicate cheeses for textural contrast.

Wafer Exhibit:

Select a variety of saltines that supplement the cheeses. Entire wheat wafers give a generous base, while water saltines offer a nonpartisan material to feature the cheddar flavors.

Plan Cheddar:

Cut the cheese into reduced-down pieces. Organize them on a serving platter, guaranteeing an outwardly engaging showcase.

Embellish Choices:

Improve the show and taste by adding corresponding components. Place groups of grapes, and a modest bunch of nuts, or shower honey over specific cheeses for added pleasantness.

Cunning Course of action:

Imaginatively place the wafers around the cheddar combination. Consider layering or stacking the cheeses for a stylishly satisfying arrangement.

Serve and Appreciate:

Your cheddar and saltines platter is fit to be delighted in! Serve it at room temperature to permit the full kinds of cheeses to sparkle.

Vegetable Spring Rolls

Planning Time: 30 minutes

Cooking Time: 15 minutes

Servings: Makes around 12 spring rolls

Fixings:

1 bundle of spring roll coverings

2 cups destroyed cabbage

1 cup julienned carrots

1 cup daintily cut chime peppers (grouped colors)

1 cup bean sprouts

1 cup meagerly cut mushrooms

3 green onions, slashed

2 cloves garlic, minced

1 tablespoon soy sauce

1 tablespoon clam sauce

1 teaspoon sesame oil

1 teaspoon ground ginger

1 tablespoon vegetable oil for sautéing

Oil for profound broiling

Bearings:

Prep the Vegetables:

In a huge wok or skillet, heat 1 tablespoon of vegetable oil.

Add garlic and ginger, sauté momentarily until fragrant.

Add cabbage, carrots, chime peppers, mushrooms, bean fledglings, and green onions. Pan-sear for 5-7 minutes until vegetables are somewhat delicate.

Preparing:

Add soy sauce, shellfish sauce, and sesame oil to the vegetables. Mix well to consolidate.

Keep on cooking for an extra 2-3 minutes. Eliminate from intensity and let the filling cool.

Get together:

Spread out a spring roll covering in a jewel shape.

Place 2-3 tablespoons of the vegetable filling in the focal point of the covering.

Crease the base corner over the filling, wrap up the sides, and roll firmly.

Fixing the Edges:

Blend a limited quantity of water with flour to shape a glue.

Seal the edges of the spring roll with the glue to keep them from opening during broiling.

Broiling:

Heat oil in a deep fryer or a huge dish to 350°F (180°C).

Cautiously place the spring rolls in the hot oil and broil until brilliant brown, turning sometimes for cooking.

Eliminate and deplete paper towels.

Serving:

Serve the vegetable spring rolls hot with your most loved plunging sauce, for example, sweet bean stew sauce or soy sauce with minced garlic.

Sustenance Data (per serving):

Calories: Around 120

Protein: 2g

Fat: 5g

Starches: 15g

Fiber: 2g

Sugar: 2g

Sodium: 300mg

Guacamole with Tortilla Chips

Fixings:

4 ready avocados

1 little red onion, finely diced

1-2 tomatoes, diced

1/4 cup new cilantro, cleaved

1-2 cloves garlic, minced

Juice of 1-2 limes

Salt and pepper to taste

Discretionary: Jalapeño, diced (for some intensity)

For serving:

Tortilla chips

Planning Time: 15 minutes

Cooking Time: 0 minutes

Servings: 4-6

Sustenance Data (per serving):

Calories: 200

Fat: 15g

Sugars: 15g

Fiber: 10g

Protein: 3g

Headings:

Set up the Avocados:

Slice the avocados down the middle, eliminate the pits, and scoop the tissue into a blending bowl.

Pound the Avocados:

Utilize a fork or potato masher to pound the avocados to your ideal consistency. Some favor stout guacamole, while others like it smoother.

Add the Aromatics:

Add the finely diced red onion, diced tomatoes, minced garlic, and cleaved cilantro to the squashed avocados.

Preparing:

Fit the juice of 1-2 limes into the combination. Season with salt and pepper to taste. For some additional kick, add diced jalapeño.

Blend Well:

Tenderly blend every one of the fixings until very much joined. Be mindful so as not to overmix; you need to keep up with the surface.

Taste and Change:

Taste the guacamole and change the lime, salt, or pepper depending on the situation. This is an ideal opportunity to make it ideal for your inclinations.

Chill (Discretionary):

While the guacamole is prepared to eat, refrigerating it for around 30 minutes permits the flavors to merge.

Serve:

Serve the guacamole in a bowl with a side of fresh tortilla chips.

Appreciate:

Jump into your hand-crafted guacamole with tortilla chips and enjoy the smooth surface and energetic flavors.

Stuffed Jalapeños

Planning Time: 15 minutes

Cooking Time: 15 minutes

Servings: 4-6

Fixings:

12 huge jalapeños

8 oz cream cheddar, relaxed

1 cup destroyed cheddar

1/2 cup cooked and disintegrated bacon

2 cloves garlic, minced

1 teaspoon onion powder

1/2 teaspoon cumin

Salt and pepper to taste

New cilantro for embellish (discretionary)

Bearings:

Preheat the Stove: Preheat your broiler to 375°F (190°C).

Get ready Jalapeños: Cut jalapeños down the middle longwise and eliminate seeds and layers. On the off chance that you favor a milder rendition, leave a few seeds for heat.

Blend Filling: In a blending bowl, consolidate relaxed cream cheddar, destroyed cheddar, bacon, minced garlic, onion powder, cumin, salt, and pepper. Blend until very much consolidated.

Stuff Jalapeños: Spoon the cream cheddar combination into each jalapeño half, it is equally filled to guarantee they.

Prepare: Put the stuffed jalapeños on a baking sheet and heat in the preheated broiler for around 15 minutes or until the jalapeños are delicate and the filling is brilliant brown.

Embellish Discretionary: Trimming with new cilantro for an explosion of flavor and variety.

Serve: Permit the stuffed jalapeños to cool somewhat before serving. They can be delighted in as a great starter or a zesty side dish.

Sustenance Data (per serving):

Calories: 180

Absolute Fat: 15g

Immersed Fat: 8g

Cholesterol: 45mg

Sodium: 280mg

Absolute Starches: 4g

Dietary Fiber: 1g

Sugars: 2g

Protein: 7g

Chapter 7:Sweet Treats

Fixings:

1 cup regular baking flour

1/2 cup unsalted margarine, mellowed

1/2 cup earthy-colored sugar, pressed

1/4 cup granulated sugar

1 enormous egg

1 teaspoon vanilla concentrate

1/2 teaspoon baking pop

1/4 teaspoon salt

1 cup chocolate chips (or your number one blend-in)

Planning Time:

15 minutes

Cooking Time:

12-15 minutes

Serving:

Makes around 24 treats

Nourishment Data (per serving):

Calories: 120

Complete Fat: 7g

Soaked Fat: 4g

Cholesterol: 20mg

Sodium: 80mg

Complete Sugars: 15g

Sugars: 10g

Protein: 1g

Bearings:

Preheat your stove to 350°F (175°C) and line a baking sheet with material paper.

In a medium-sized bowl, cream together the mellowed margarine, earthy-colored sugar, and granulated sugar until light and cushy.

Add the egg and vanilla concentrate to the blend, beating great until completely joined.

In a different bowl, whisk together the flour, baking pop, and salt.

Slowly add the dry fixings to the wet fixings, blending until a smooth treat mixture structures.

Tenderly overlap in the chocolate chips or your picked blend in until uniformly conveyed all through the batter.

Drop adjusted tablespoons of mixture onto the pre-arranged baking sheet, leaving adequate room between every treat.

Prepare in the preheated stove for 12-15 minutes or until the edges are brilliant brown.

Permit the treats to cool on the baking sheet for a couple of moments before moving them to a wire rack to totally cool.

Once cooled, enjoy these grand sweet treats!

Chocolate Avocado Mousse

Planning Time: 15 minutes

Cooking Time: 0 minutes

Serving: 4 servings

Enjoying a rich and velvety chocolate treat doesn't need to think twice about well-being. Enter Chocolate Avocado Mousse - a faultless joy that joins the debauchery of chocolate with the wholesome advantages of avocados.

Fixings:

2 ready avocados

1/3 cup cocoa powder

1/4 cup maple syrup or honey

1/4 cup almond milk (or any milk of your decision)

1 teaspoon vanilla concentrate

A spot of salt

Headings:

Plan Avocados: Scoop out the tissue of the ready avocados and spot them in a blender or food processor.

Add Cocoa Powder: Integrate the cocoa powder into the blender, guaranteeing a smooth mix.

Improve It Up: Pour in the maple syrup or honey to add the ideal measure of pleasantness.

Mix Smooth: Mix the blend until it accomplishes a smooth consistency, scratching the sides if essential.

Fluid Enchantment: Present the almond milk (or your favored milk) to make a tasty, velvety surface.

Upgrade Flavor: Drop in the vanilla concentrate and a spot of salt. Mix again to completely join every one of the fixings.

Chill and Serve: Move the mousse into individual serving bowls or glasses. Refrigerate for no less than 2 hours to permit it to solidify.

Embellish (Discretionary): Before serving, you can add a sprinkle of cocoa powder, ground chocolate, or new berries for an additional dash of flavor and style.

Sustenance Data (per serving):

Calories: 200

Fat: 15g

Sugars: 18g

Fiber: 7g

Protein: 3g

Keto Air Fryer Doughnuts

Fixings:

2 cups almond flour

1/2 cup granulated erythritol (or your favored keto-accommodating sugar)

2 tsp baking powder

1/2 tsp cinnamon

1/4 tsp salt

3 huge eggs

1/2 cup unsweetened almond milk

1 tsp vanilla concentrate

1/4 cup dissolved coconut oil

Planning Time:

15 minutes

Cooking Time:

10 minutes

Serving:

Makes roughly 12 doughnuts

Bearings:

Preheat Air Fryer:

Preheat your air fryer to 350°F (180°C).

Blend Dry Fixings:

In a blending bowl, consolidate almond flour, erythritol, baking powder, cinnamon, and salt. Blend well to guarantee even appropriation of fixings.

Add Wet Fixings:

In a different bowl, whisk together eggs, almond milk, vanilla concentrate, and softened coconut oil. Empty the wet fixings into the dry fixings and mix until a smooth player structures.

Fill Doughnut Molds:

Oil your air fryer doughnut molds with a touch of coconut oil. Spoon the hitter into each shape, filling it around 66% full.

Air Fry:

Place the filled molds into the preheated air fryer crate. Air fry at 350°F (180°C) for roughly 8-10 minutes or until the doughnuts are brilliant brown and a toothpick embedded tells the truth.

Cool and Coating (Discretionary):

Permit the doughnuts to cool in the molds for a couple of moments before moving them to a wire rack. Alternatively, you can frost the doughnuts with a keto-accommodating frosting produced using powdered erythritol and a hint of almond milk.

Nourishment Data (per serving, without coat):

Calories: 120

Absolute Fat: 10g

Soaked Fat: 4g

Cholesterol: 40mg

Sodium: 120mg

Absolute Carbs: 4g

Dietary Fiber: 2g

Sugars: 1g

Protein: 5g

Berry Almond Fresh

Planning Time: 15 minutes

Cooking Time: 40 minutes

Servings: 6-8

Fixings:

4 cups blended berries (strawberries, blueberries, raspberries)

1/2 cup granulated sugar

2 tablespoons cornstarch

1 tablespoon lemon juice

1 cup outdated moved oats

1/2 cup cut almonds

1/2 cup regular baking flour

1/2 cup pressed earthy colored sugar

1/2 teaspoon ground cinnamon

1/4 teaspoon salt

1/2 cup unsalted margarine, cold and cut into little shapes

Bearings:

Preheat Stove: Preheat your broiler to 350°F (175°C) and oil a baking dish.

Get ready Berries: In an enormous bowl, delicately throw together the blended berries, granulated sugar, cornstarch, and lemon juice until the berries are equally covered. Move the berry combination to the lubed baking dish.

Make Fresh Garnish: In a different bowl, consolidate moved oats, cut almonds, flour, earthy-colored sugar, cinnamon, and salt. Add the virus spread 3D squares and utilize your fingers to integrate the margarine into the dry fixings until the combination looks like coarse scraps.

Top the Berries: Equally sprinkle the fresh garnish over the berry blend in the baking dish, covering the berries.

Prepare: Spot the baking dish in the preheated broiler and heat for 35-40 minutes, or until the fixing is brilliant brown and the berry filling is rising around the edges.

Cool and Serve: Permit the berry almond fresh to cool for a couple of moments before serving. Serve it warm, and consider adding a scoop of vanilla frozen yogurt or a spot of whipped cream for an additional treat.

Sustenance Data (per serving):

Note: Dietary benefits might change in light of explicit fixings utilized.

Calories: 320

Absolute Fat: 16g

Soaked Fat: 7g

Cholesterol: 30mg

Sodium: 75mg

Absolute Starches: 45g

Dietary Fiber: 5g

Sugars: 26g

Protein: 4g

Chocolate chip treats

Fixings:

1 cup unsalted spread, relaxed

1 cup granulated sugar

1 cup earthy colored sugar, stuffed

2 huge eggs

1 teaspoon vanilla concentrate

3 cups regular flour

1 teaspoon baking pop

1/2 teaspoon baking powder

1/2 teaspoon salt

2 cups semisweet chocolate chips

Planning Time: 15 minutes

Cooking Time: 10-12 minutes

Servings: Roughly 36 treats

Bearings:

Preheat the Stove:

Preheat your stove to 350°F (175°C) and line baking sheets with material paper.

Cream Spread and Sugars:

In a huge bowl, cream together the relaxed margarine, granulated sugar, and earthy colored sugar until smooth and cushy.

Add Eggs and Vanilla:

Beat in the eggs each in turn, then, at that point, mix in the vanilla concentrate.

Consolidate Dry Fixings:

In a different bowl, whisk together the flour, baking pop, baking powder, and salt.

Blend Wet and Dry Fixings:

Bit by bit add the dry fixings to the wet fixings, blending until recently consolidated. Be careful not to overmix.

Overlap in Chocolate Chips:

Tenderly crease in the chocolate chips until uniformly appropriate all through the treat mixture.

Scoop and Prepare:

Utilizing a treat scoop or spoon, drop adjusted tablespoons of batter onto the pre-arranged baking sheets, leaving sufficient room between every treat.

Heat Flawlessly:

Heat in the preheated broiler for 10-12 minutes or until the edges are brilliant brown. The focuses may appear to be marginally underdone, yet they will solidify as they cool.

Cool and Appreciate:

Permit the treats to cool on the baking sheets for a couple of moments before moving them to wire racks to totally cool.

Nourishment Data (per serving, given 36 servings):

Calories: 180

Complete Fat: 9g

Soaked Fat: 5g

Cholesterol: 25mg

Sodium: 80mg

Complete Starches: 24g

Sugars: 15g

Protein: 2g

Strawberry shortcake

Planning Time: 20 minutes

Cooking Time: 15 minutes

Serving: 6 servings

Fixings:

2 cups new strawberries, cut

1/4 cup granulated sugar

2 1/3 cups regular flour

1/4 cup granulated sugar (for shortcakes)

1 tablespoon baking powder

1/2 teaspoon salt

1/2 cup unsalted spread, cold, and cut into little pieces

1 cup milk

1 teaspoon vanilla concentrate

1 cup heavy cream

2 tablespoons powdered sugar

Bearings:

Set up the Strawberries: In a bowl, consolidate cut strawberries with 1/4 cup of sugar. Mix well and allow it to sit for no less than 15 minutes to permit the strawberries to deliver their juices.

Preheat Stove: Preheat the broiler to 425°F (220°C).

Make the Shortcakes: In a huge blending bowl, whisk together the flour, 1/4 cup sugar, baking powder, and salt. Add cold margarine pieces and utilize a cake shaper or your fingers to cut the spread into the dry fixings until the combination looks like coarse scraps.

Add Wet Fixings: Pour in the milk and vanilla concentrate. Mix until recently consolidated. Don't overmix.

Structure Shortcakes: Turn the batter out onto a gently floured surface. Tenderly pat it into a 1-inch thick square shape. Utilize a round roll shaper to remove shortcakes. Put them on a baking sheet fixed with material paper.

Prepare: Heat for 12-15 minutes or until the shortcakes are brilliant brown. Permit them to cool on a wire rack.

Whip the Cream: In a chilled bowl, whip the heavy cream and powdered sugar until firm pinnacles structure.

Collect: Cut every shortcake in half on a level plane. Spoon a liberal measure of macerated strawberries onto the base half, add a touch of whipped cream, and afterward place the top portion of the shortcake on top.

Serve Enhancement with extra strawberries and a cleaning of powdered sugar whenever wanted. Serve right away and partake in your custom-made strawberry shortcake!

Nourishment Data (per serving):

Calories: 380

Absolute Fat: 21g

Soaked Fat: 13g

Cholesterol: 65mg

Sodium: 330mg

Absolute Sugars: 43g

Dietary Fiber: 2g

Sugars: 15g

Protein:5g

Vanilla ice cream

Planning Time: 15 minutes

Cooking Time: 25-30 minutes

Serving: 6-8 servings

Fixings:

2 cups heavy cream

1 cup entire milk

3/4 cup granulated sugar

1 tablespoon unadulterated vanilla concentrate

Touch of salt

Bearings:

In a blending bowl, whisk together the weighty cream, entire milk, granulated sugar, vanilla concentrate, and a touch of salt until the sugar breaks down totally.

Empty the blend into a frozen yogurt producer, adhering to the maker's guidelines. Beat the combination until it arrives at a delicate serve consistency.

Move the semi-frozen yogurt into a lidded holder, spreading it uniformly. Cover the surface with material paper before fixing with the top; this keeps ice precious stones from framing.

Freeze the frozen yogurt for no less than 4 hours or short-term for a firmer surface.

Before serving, let the frozen yogurt sit at room temperature for a couple of moments to mellow. Scoop into bowls or cones and partake in the velvety decency of hand-crafted vanilla frozen yogurt.

Nourishment Data (per serving, expecting 8 servings):

Calories: 320

Fat: 25g

Soaked Fat: 15g

Cholesterol: 90mg

Sodium: 40mg

Starches: 20g

Sugars: 18g

Protein: 3g

Caramel brownies

Planning Time: 15 minutes

Cooking Time: 25-30 minutes

Servings: 12 brownies

Fixings:

1 cup unsalted spread

2 cups granulated sugar

4 huge eggs

1 teaspoon vanilla concentrate

1 cup regular baking flour

1/2 cup cocoa powder

1/4 teaspoon salt

1 cup caramel sauce (natively constructed or locally acquired)

1/2 cup chocolate chips (discretionary, for additional extravagance)

Headings:

Preheat the Broiler:

Preheat your broiler to 350°F (175°C). Oil a 9x13-inch baking skillet or line it with material paper.

Set up the Player:

In a microwave-safe bowl, liquefy the margarine. Add sugar and mix until very much joined. Beat in the eggs, each in turn, and afterward add the vanilla concentrate.

Join Dry Fixings:

In a different bowl, whisk together the flour, cocoa powder, and salt. Step by step add the dry fixings to the wet fixings, blending until recently joined. Be mindful so as not to overmix.

Layering the Integrity:

Pour half of the brownie player into the pre-arranged container. Sprinkle half of the caramel sauce over the hitter. Rehash with the excess hitter and caramel sauce. Whirl the layers with a blade for a marbled impact. If you're feeling additionally debauched, sprinkle chocolate chips on top.

Prepare Flawlessly:

Prepare in the preheated stove for 25-30 minutes or until a toothpick embedded into the middle emerges with sodden pieces (not wet player). Keep in mind, it's smarter to somewhat underbake than overbake for that gooey surface.

Cool and Cut:

Permit the brownies to cool in the prospect for 15-20 minutes. Then, move them to a wire rack to cool them before cutting them into squares.

Sustenance Data (per serving):

Calories: 380

All out Fat: 20g

Immersed Fat: 12g

Cholesterol: 105mg

Sodium: 90mg

All out Sugars: 48g

Dietary Fiber: 2g

Sugars: 35g

Protein: 4g

Chapter 8: Condiments and Sauces

1. Exemplary Ketchup:

Planning Time: 10 minutes

Cooking Time: 30 minutes

Serving: Makes around 2 cups

Fixings: Tomatoes, vinegar, sugar, onion, garlic, salt, and flavors.

Bearings: Stew tomatoes, onions, and garlic, then, at that point, mix with vinegar, sugar, and flavors. Cook until thickened.

2. Tart Mustard:

Planning Time: 5 minutes

Cooking Time: No cooking required

Serving: Yields 1 cup

Fixings: Mustard seeds, vinegar, water, salt, and discretionary flavors.

Bearings: Splash mustard seeds in a combination of vinegar and water, mix, add salt, and tweak with flavors whenever you want.

3. Rich Mayonnaise:

Planning Time: 5 minutes

Cooking Time: No cooking required

Serving: Makes 1 cup

Fixings: Egg yolk, Dijon mustard, lemon juice, oil, salt, and pepper.

Headings: Whisk together egg yolk, mustard, and lemon juice. Gradually add oil while rushing until velvety. Season with salt and pepper.

4. Lively bar-b-que Sauce:

Planning Time: 10 minutes

Cooking Time: 20 minutes

Serving: Yields roughly 2 cups

Fixings: Ketchup, earthy colored sugar, vinegar, Worcestershire sauce, mustard, flavors.

Bearings: Join all fixings in a pot, and stew until flavors merge, and the sauce thickens.

5. New Salsa:

Planning Time: 15 minutes

Cooking Time: No cooking required

Serving: Makes 2 cups

Fixings: Tomatoes, onion, cilantro, jalapeño, lime juice, salt.

Headings: Dice tomatoes, onion, and jalapeño. Blend in with slashed cilantro, lime squeeze, and salt.

Nourishment Data:

Toppings and sauces can add flavor without numerous calories.

Use balance to control sodium and sugar consumption.

Avocado Lime Aioli

Fixings:

1 ready avocado

2 cloves garlic, minced

1/4 cup mayonnaise

1 tablespoon Dijon mustard

Juice of 2 limes

1/4 cup olive oil

Salt and pepper to taste

Bearings:

Set up the Avocado: Cut the ready avocado down the middle, eliminate the pit, and scoop the tissue into a bowl.

Crush Avocado: Squash the avocado with a fork until smooth.

Add Garlic: Add minced garlic to the crushed avocado and blend well.

Consolidate Mayonnaise and Mustard: Mix in mayonnaise and Dijon mustard until the blend is smooth and all around joined.

Press in Lime Juice: Get the juice of 2 limes into the bowl, guaranteeing a citrusy punch to the aioli.

Shower Olive Oil: Steadily sprinkle in the olive oil while constantly blending to emulsify the fixings.

Season to Taste: Season the aioli with salt and pepper as per your inclination. Blend well.

Chill (Discretionary): For a marginally thicker consistency, refrigerate the aioli for 30 minutes before serving.

Sustenance Data (per serving):

Note: Dietary benefits might differ in light of explicit fixings utilized.

Calories: around 120

Fat: 11g

Immersed Fat: 1.5g

Cholesterol: 5mg

Sodium: 110mg

Starches: 5g

Fiber: 3g

Sugar: 0.5g

Protein: 1g

Serving:

This recipe yields around 1 cup of avocado lime aioli. A serving size is ordinarily 2 tablespoons.

Planning Time:

15 minutes

Cooking Time:

N/A (No cooking required)

Sans sugar bar-b-que Sauce

Fixings:

1 cup pureed tomatoes (unsweetened)

1/4 cup apple juice vinegar

1 tablespoon Worcestershire sauce (search for sans sugar choices)

1 teaspoon smoked paprika

1 teaspoon garlic powder

1 teaspoon onion powder

1/2 teaspoon dark pepper

1/2 teaspoon mustard powder

1/4 teaspoon cayenne pepper (conform to taste)

Fluid stevia or erythritol to taste

Planning Time: 10 minutes

Cooking Time: 20 minutes

Servings: Roughly 8 (2-tablespoon servings)

Bearings:

In a pot, consolidate the pureed tomatoes, apple juice vinegar, and Worcestershire sauce over medium intensity.

Mix in the smoked paprika, garlic powder, onion powder, dark pepper, mustard powder, and cayenne pepper.

Permit the blend to come to a delicate stew, then, at that point, diminish the intensity to low.

Allow the sauce to stew for around 15-20 minutes, blending every so often to abstain from consuming.

Taste the sauce and change the pleasantness with fluid stevia or erythritol as per your inclination.

When the sauce arrives at your ideal consistency and flavor, eliminate it from intensity and let it cool.

Nourishment Data (per 2-tablespoon serving):

Calories: 15

Absolute Fat: 0g

Cholesterol: 0mg

Sodium: 120mg

Absolute Starches: 3g

Dietary Fiber: 1g

Sugars: 0g

Protein: 1g

Tips:

Explore different avenues regarding the pleasantness level to track down the ideal equilibrium for your taste.

Store the sans sugar bar-b-que sauce in a hermetically sealed holder in the cooler for as long as about fourteen days.

Garlic Spice Margarine

Planning Time: 10 minutes

Cooking Time: 0 minutes

Serving: Around 8 tablespoons

Fixings:

1 cup (2 sticks) unsalted margarine, relaxed

4 cloves garlic, minced

2 tablespoons new parsley, finely cleaved

1 tablespoon new chives, cleaved

1 teaspoon new thyme leaves

1 teaspoon new rosemary, finely slashed

Salt and dark pepper to taste

Headings:

Plan Fixings: Guarantee that the margarine is mellowed at room temperature for simple blending. Mince the garlic, slash the new spices, and put them away.

Blend Margarine and Garlic: In a blending bowl, join the mellowed spread and minced garlic. Utilize a spatula or blender to mix them until the garlic is equally conveyed all through the spread.

Add Spices: Integrate the cleaved parsley, chives, thyme, and rosemary into the margarine blend. Mix well to guarantee the spices are uniformly scattered.

Season: Season the garlic spice margarine with salt and dark pepper as indicated by your taste inclinations. Blend again to completely consolidate every one of the fixings.

Shape and Refrigerate: Put a sheet of saran wrap on the counter and move the enhanced spread combination onto it. Shape the margarine into a log or spot it in a holder. Wrap it firmly with the saran wrap and refrigerate for somewhere around 2 hours or until firm.

Serve: When the garlic spice margarine has cemented, it's prepared to utilize. Cut it into segments or scoop out depending on the situation. Use it to improve the kind of different dishes like barbecued meats, and cooked vegetables, or just spread it on bread.

Sustenance Data (per tablespoon):

Calories: 102

Complete Fat: 11g

Soaked Fat: 7g

Cholesterol: 30mg

Sodium: 0.5mg

Complete Carbs: 0.3g

Protein: 0.2g

uce

Fixings:

1 cup soybeans

1 cup wheat berries

4 cups water

1 cup ocean salt

1 tablespoon koji spores (accessible in specialty stores)

Planning Time: 24 hours (for splashing soybeans and wheat berries)

Cooking Time: a half year (maturation)

Serving: Roughly 2 cups

Nourishment Data (per tablespoon):

Calories: 10

Complete Fat: 0g

Sodium: 1,000mg

Complete Carbs: 2g

Protein: 1g

Bearings:

Splash the Soybeans and Wheat Berries:

Wash 1 cup of soybeans and 1 cup of wheat berries completely.

Absorb them 4 cups of water for 24 hours to mellow.

Cook the Soybeans and Wheat Berries:

Channel the splashed soybeans and wheat berries.

Place them in a huge pot and add 4 cups of water.

Heat to the point of boiling and afterward stew for 3 hours until the beans and wheat are delicate.

Get ready for Koji Culture:

While the soybeans and wheat are cooking, blend 1 tablespoon of koji spores with a limited quantity of water to make a glue.

When the soybeans and wheat are cooked, cool them to around 122°F (50°C) and blend in the koji glue.

Aging:

Move the blend to a spotless, disinfected holder.

Cover it freely to consider airflow and aging.

Place the compartment in a warm, dim spot for quite some time, blending once in a while.

Strain and Add Salt:

Following a half year, strain the blend to eliminate solids.

Mix in 1 cup of ocean salt until it breaks up.

Age the Soy Sauce:

Permit the soy sauce to progress in years for an extra month, putting away it in a cool, dull spot.

Bottle and Appreciate:

When matured, bottle the soy sauce and refrigerate.

Utilize this natively constructed soy sauce to lift the kinds of your #1 dishes.

Chapter 9:
Troubleshooting and
Tips

Investigating is the precise course of distinguishing, examining, and settling issues or issues that might happen in different frameworks, gadgets, or cycles. Whether it's a failing electronic gadget, programming error, or functional test, viable investigating requires an intelligent and purposeful methodology.

Key Stages in Investigating:

Recognize the Issue: Characterize the issue or side effect. Accumulate significant data to comprehend the unique circumstances and any new changes that may be connected.

Disconnect the Reason: Separate the framework or cycle into parts to pinpoint the wellspring of the issue. Use testing or symptomatic instruments to limit prospects.

Foster Arrangements: When the main driver is distinguished, investigate expected arrangements. Consider the most effective and down-to-earth ways to deal with and address the issue.

Execute Fixes: Apply the selected arrangement cautiously. It might include adjusting settings, refreshing programming, supplanting parts, or following explicit methods.

Check Goal: In the wake of carrying out the arrangement, confirm if the issue is settled. Testing and checking are vital to guarantee that the fix is successful.

Tips for Powerful Investigating:

Documentation: Keep itemized records of framework designs, changes, and investigating steps. This data can be important for future reference.

Keep even-headed and Deliberate: Investigating can be testing, yet staying totally under control and following an orderly methodology will improve the probability of progress.

Update Programming and Firmware: Guarantee that all applicable programming and firmware are cutting-edge. Makers frequently discharge refreshes that address known issues.

Check for Client Mistakes: at times, issues might emerge from client blunders. Check that clients are adhering to directions accurately and know about legitimate techniques.

Team up and Look for Info: Draw in with partners or online networks for counsel. Alternate points of view can give important bits of knowledge and arrangements.

Reinforcement Frameworks: Before carrying out fixes, back up basic information or framework arrangements. This prudent step forestalls potential information misfortune during the investigation.

Utilize Symptomatic Devices: Influence worked in analytic apparatuses or outsider utilities to productively recognize and dissect more.

Figure out the Framework: Foster a profound comprehension of the frameworks you investigate.

Information on how parts collaborate can assist the investigating system.

By following these investigating standards and tips, people can improve their capacity to recognize and determine issues across many frameworks and innovations. Effective investigating settles prompt issues as well as adds to continuous framework enhancement and unwavering quality.

Normal Air Fryer Issues

Lopsided Cooking: One common issue is lopsided cooking, where certain pieces of the food may be overcooked while others remain half-cooked. This could be expected due to congestion or unpredictable food position in the air fryer bushel.

Food Adhering to the Container: A few clients experience issues with food adhering to the air fryer crate, bringing about a chaotic and lopsided cook. Appropriately lubing the bin or utilizing material paper can assist with reducing this issue.

Smoke Creation: Unreasonable smoke during cooking is a worry for some clients. This can be brought about by an abundance of oil or fat trickling onto the warming component. Standard cleaning and keeping away from excessively greasy food varieties can limit smoke.

Unsavory Scents: Certain air fryers might produce terrible scents, particularly during the underlying purposes. This is frequently ascribed to assembling deposits. Running the machine void for a brief period can assist with disposing of these smells.

Wrong Temperature and Timing: Some air fryers may not keep up with precise temperature settings or cooking times. Utilizing a stove thermometer to confirm temperature and changing cooking times depending on the situation can assist with guaranteeing exact cooking.

Uproarious Activity: Unnecessary clamor during activity can be annoying. Normal upkeep, like cleaning the fan and eliminating any flotsam and jetsam, can add to a calmer presentation.

Buildup Development: Buildup can collect in the air fryer, prompting saturated results. Guaranteeing food is dry before cooking and permitting the air fryer to preheat satisfactorily can assist with alleviating this issue.

Computerized Show Glitches: Issues with the advanced presentation, like glinting or not showing precise data, can happen. Checking for free associations, guaranteeing appropriate power supply, and counseling the producer's investigating guide might assist with settling these issues.

Chipping Covering: Some air fryer crates have a non-stick covering that might start to piece after some time. Utilizing non-grating cleaning apparatuses and observing the maker's cleaning rules can assist with keeping up with the honesty of the covering.

Scent Move Between Food Sources: areas of strength for cooking food sources continuously may bring about flavors moving between dishes. It's prudent to clean the air fryer completely between various sorts of food sources to forestall flavor pollution.

Fixing Replacements

Fixing replacements can be critical expertise in the kitchen, empowering cooks to adjust recipes in light of accessibility, dietary limitations, or individual inclinations. Understanding the properties of fixings is fundamental for fruitful replacements. For instance, trading spread for oil in baking or utilizing yogurt rather than acrid cream can influence the surface and kind of the last dish.

Normal replacements incorporate involving fruit purée or pounded bananas as egg swaps in baking for a vegetarian choice, or subbing buttermilk with a combination of milk and vinegar. While subbing fixings, consider flavor profiles, surfaces, and dampness content to keep up with the honesty of the dish.

It's vital to take note that a few replacements may not work consistently in all recipes. Trial and error and experience with the particular attributes of fixings are critical. Also, people with dietary limitations or sensitivities frequently depend on replacements to satisfy their necessities, for example, utilizing sans-gluten flour or dairy choices.

Monitoring fixing replacements improves culinary flexibility as well as energizes imagination in the kitchen. Whether driven by need or longing to try, excelling at fixing replacements engages cooks to change recipes while accomplishing flavorful outcomes unhesitatingly.

Conclusion

Support for Your Keto Air Fryer Excursion

Setting out on a Keto Air Fryer venture is an estimable decision for those looking for a better way of life. The mix of the ketogenic diet's low-carb approach and the comfort of an air fryer makes a strong pair. As you explore this way, recollect that support is an essential sidekick.

First and foremost, commend your triumphs, regardless of how little. Each effectively arranged keto-accommodating air-seared dinner is a stage toward your objectives. Perceive the work you put into picking healthy fixings and excelling at air searing, cultivating a feeling of achievement.

Remain inquisitive and daring in your culinary investigations. The universe of keto-accommodating recipes for the air fryer is huge. Explore different avenues regarding different flavors, marinades, and cooking strategies to keep your taste buds invigorated. This changes up your feasts as well as builds up your obligation to the excursion.

Tolerance is key in any groundbreaking cycle. Comprehend that adjusting to a ketogenic way of life and becoming capable of air broiling takes time. Permit yourself the space to learn, commit errors, and develop. Progress will be progress, regardless of the speed.

Encircle yourself with a steady local area. Whether it's internet-based discussions, virtual entertainment gatherings, or loved ones, having an organization that shares your objectives can give inspiration, tips, and a feeling of fellowship. Share your triumphs and difficulties, and draw motivation from the encounters of others.

Ultimately, focus on taking care of oneself. Supporting your body goes past food; it incorporates satisfactory rest, hydration, and care. A balanced way to deal with health upgrades the positive effect of your keto air fryer venture on both your physical and mental prosperity.

In synopsis, consolation for your keto air fryer venture includes recognizing accomplishments, embracing culinary investigation, rehearsing persistence, encouraging a steady local area, and focusing on all-encompassing taking care of oneself. Remember these perspectives as you relish the advantages of a better way of life through the combination of keto standards and air-searing procedures.

Printed in Great Britain
by Amazon

35299815R00155